crystals

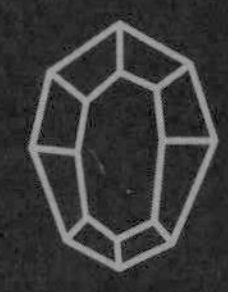
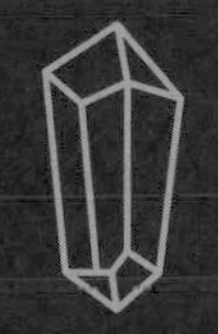

IN FOCUS
WORKBOOK

crystals

A Personal Guide to the Power of Crystals

REGINA M. BRESLER

WELLFLEET PRESS

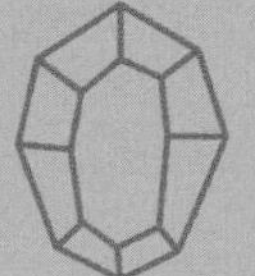

contents

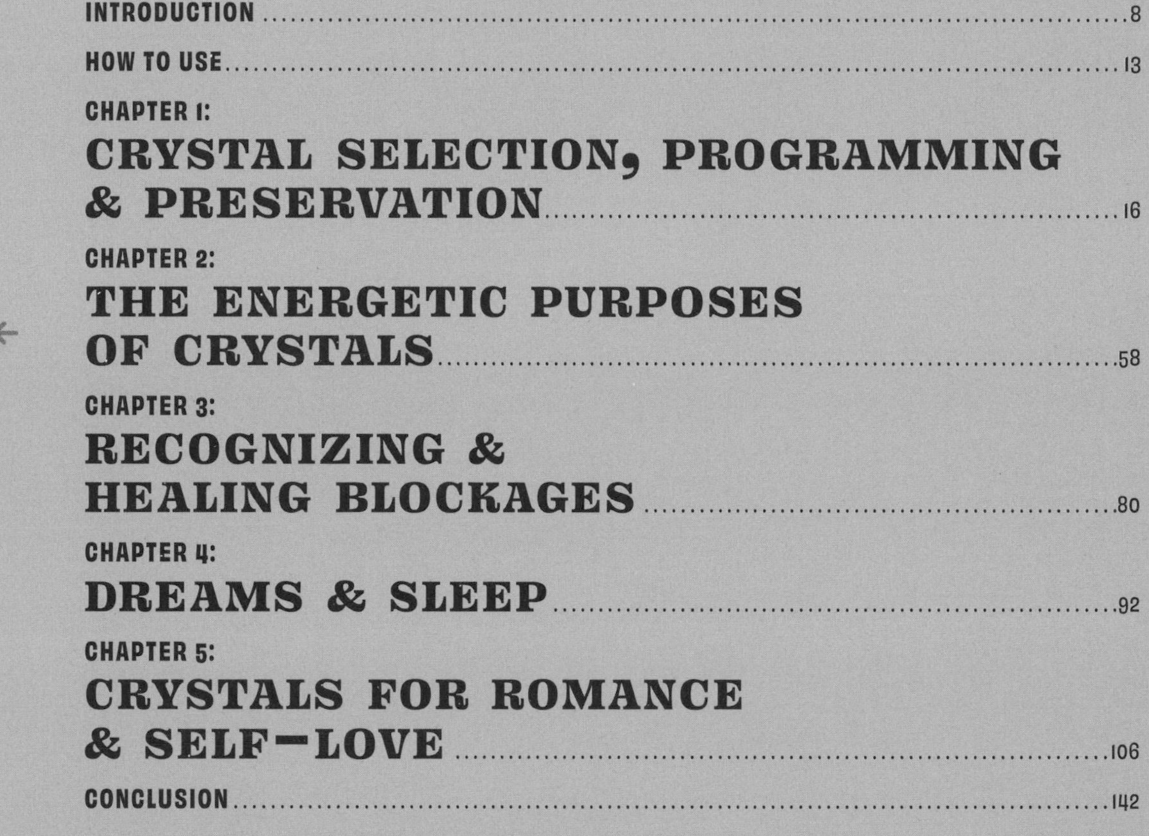

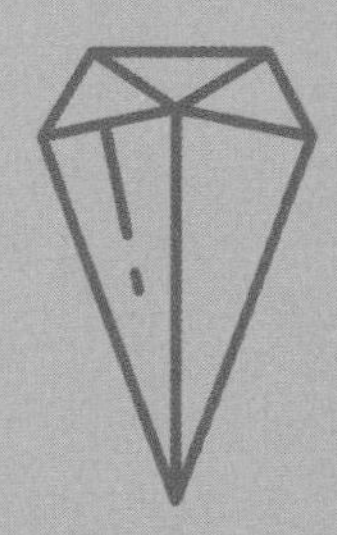

introduction

WHAT ARE CRYSTALS?

Let's start by taking a few moments to reflect on what drew you to the book you are holding: the very tangible and geologically definable, yet utterly mystifying beauty and magic of crystals and minerals. Sometimes dismissed as a fad, a fashionable vein of spirituality, or a design element, these striking earthly delights have grown among us, and long before us. They've inspired engineers, artists, and spiritualists of every variety. But what power do they possess, and how should they be utilized?

Composed of atoms that create unmistakable patterns, and an example of the sacred geometry of nature, crystals fall under seven specific forms: Isometric (cubic), hexagonal, monoclinic (prism-shaped), orthorhombic (conjoined pyramids), tetragonal (rectangular), triclinic (abstract forms), and trigonal (rectangular with triangle ends). Some may require a trained eye, or even a microscope, to identify, but recognizing these structures (or, at the very least, their existence) could clue you into what has drawn everyone from mystics to mathematically minded engineers to fixate on these earthly treasures. These crystal structures form complex mineral compositions, not to be confused with rocks, which are composed of multitudes of minerals and lack a clear structure. While collectors might colloquially be referred to as "rock hounds," knowing this distinction should clarify why calling their revered and cherished specimens "rocks" feels like a slur.

There are currently thousands of known crystal compositions, the most common and prevalent of which is quartz. Quartz is perhaps the most classic image that comes to mind when the word crystal is mentioned. With its glassy, jagged clusters and individual spears that range in size from microscopic pin to epic pillar, quartz covers roughly 12 percent of the Earth's surface, and 20 percent of its crust. Found on every continent and across the color spectrum, quartz is a nearly pure chemical compound holding constant physical properties, birthed from the union of two of our most abundant chemical elements: oxygen and silicon. It's no surprise then that silicates, the mineralogical group that quartz belongs to, appear in more than 90 percent of rock-forming crystals.

Quartz is often the entry point for collectors and an easily accessible gateway for future crystal fiends. It may start small: a tumbled pebble embedded in a candle, a single point strung on a necklace, or perhaps a small cluster you find at a museum gift shop that makes you feel like you're watching a rainstorm frozen in time. You might believe that an "ideal" specimen is one that has no structural flaws or impurities, until you encounter one that contains rutile (titanium dioxide), with wispy hairs of gold and red that fill out this "eternal ice" (it once was believed to be fossilized ice sent from the gods). As you begin to examine pieces more closely, you'll find yourself delighted when you encounter your first enhydro agate, a bubble of water or unsolidified quartz that became trapped during the formation of the crystal. Did the gods forget to check their freezer settings?

Environmental conditions and trace elemental inclusions determine these formations and foster nearly endless variants to study and discover. Mineraloids, however, are an exception to the crystal categorization rules. Although not technically crystal formations, these can be powerful tools and are beloved by collectors and energy workers alike. Technically speaking, these aren't crystals or minerals, they are mineral-like without meeting the elemental requirements. Many are glass, animal, plant-based, or even liquid, and they are widely considered to be quite powerful: Think obsidian in its many forms. Often known as truth amplifiers and strong psychic shields from negativity, mineraloids enhance creativity and healthy emotion, and help release psychic wounds. Amber is a good example—it is thought to be one of the oldest healing stones, and is said to promote self-confidence and absorb negative energy. Or moldavite, a tektite which formed when a meteor hit Earth (or perhaps a variety of lunar obsidian, the debate remains), has a reputation for initiating rapid spiritual evolution and activating chakras. These examples only scratch the surface. Geology goes deep, both literally and figuratively!

So why, then, does uttering the word "crystals" in mixed company often elicit eyerolls from skeptics who associate the term strictly with New Age trends and little else? Is it truly so hard to imagine that something so scientifically rooted, tangible, and fundamental to our environment—that powers our electronics, filters our water and air, and provides pigments for everything from our clothes to our cosmetics—could also harness energy that can be applied to our metaphysical needs? Attempting to disprove the magic and the eons of lore accompanying it is always an option, but the conversation about crystals is an ancient one, spanning space and time. Metaphysical manifestations and concrete evidence prove the dynamic nature of this enchanting part of our world.

COMMON MINERALOIDS

Opal	Moldavite	Amber
Obsidian	Pearl	Anthracite

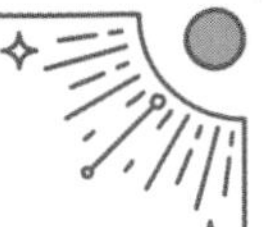

CRYSTAL CLASSIFICATION SYSTEMS

SYSTEM	SHAPE	COMMON EXAMPLES
Isometric		Garnet, diamond, fluorite, lapis lazuli
Trigonal		Ruby, quartz, calcite, agate, jasper
Hexagonal		Calcite, quartz, emerald, graphite, tourmaline
Tetragonal		Anatase, apophyllite, zircon, scapolite
Orthorhombic		Aragonite, topaz, peridot, celestite
Monoclinic		Gypsum, jadeite, azurite, muscovite
Triclinic		Turquoise, labrodite, rhodonite, kyanite

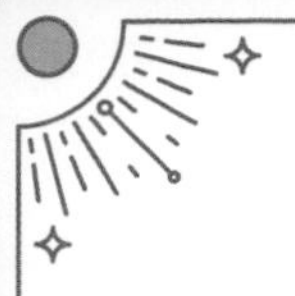

CRYSTALS IN HUMAN CULTURE

While not everyone may recognize or agree upon their significance, crystals have been featured in human life since the dawn of civilization. Employed in the ornamentation of protective amulets and ceremonial objects, lapis lazuli graced relics dating as far back as 7000 BCE in Mesopotamia and were marks of divinity, bringing healing energy and luck. The equally revered turquoise had a potent reputation for protective energy and preserving health among some tribes of the Indigenous Peoples of the Americas. Shiva stone, specifically banalingam (meaning "the self-existent mark or sign of God"), is held sacred among Hindus and devotees of the god Shiva. Known to form only in the Narmada River (one of India's seven holy sites), the stones are held as an iconic symbol of divinity. They naturally form in an oblong shape said to awaken Kundalini energy and are representative of the cosmic egg from which all life hatched.

Aaron's breastplate, a piece of priestly armor referenced in the Book of Exodus, was an intricate adornment also known as the Breastplate of Judgment and employed as an oracle in the high temple. It featured an array of twelve stones. Depending on which religious scholar's interpretation you trust, the stones were laid out in three columns and four rows and included lapis lazuli, turquoise, carnelian, peridot (or topaz), emerald, sapphire, amethyst, garnet, agate, quartz (or diamond), aquamarine, and jasper. Each gem represented one of the Twelve Tribes of Israel and is said to be the basis of what we now call birthstones.

The list goes on. From the anchoring points of Druid altars and intricate inlays of Buddhist relics to the tools of Reiki practitioners and the jewelry of Vedic astrologers, crystals always find a way to enter the conversation. The lore of crystals exists in the mythology of early civilizations, cross-culturally and on every continent, and are quite literally part of the bedrock of our world. It is no surprise that they've kept a hold on the human imagination since we first learned how to harvest them from the earth.

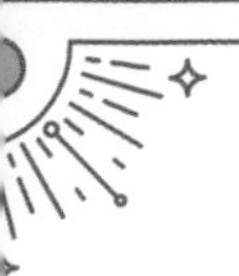

HOW TO USE THIS BOOK

In the chapters to follow, I will help you learn about crystals and the intricate energies that can help empower and beautify your life. At the beginning of the chapters and ahead of each topic's exercises you will be provided with foundational information and instruction. We will dive deeply into different crystal varieties, their personalities and energies, their properties, and how to best use each in such a way that you will extract maximum benefit. You will learn to recognize which crystals you need in any given situation, how to use crystals to form a relationship with your higher self, and how to infuse them into your life for maintenance of peace and joy.

Since a large portion of crystal knowledge is intuitive, it can be a little difficult to keep track of which crystals work for you in specific instances, so I will teach you how to keep crystal logs to keep track of which stones you most connect with. You will encounter writing exercises and journaling prompts that will help you sort out your thoughts and feelings and assist you in focusing on what your actual energetic needs are, rather than running on pure emotion. Guided meditations, with pre- and post-meditative prompts, will help you lower your anxiety and raise your energetic vibrations. You will cleanse your space, your tools, and your crystals so that you can receive the highest level of power from your practice. We will even bring crystals outside to your garden and use them to nurture your plants! We close the book with self-care strategies and loving yourself, which is where your own power lives.

The goal of this workbook is to help you build on each concept in a way that enables you to harness the beauty, meaning, and power behind each magical crystal, and to help you apply these mystical properties to your advantage. Thank you for joining me here and granting me permission to teach about this beautiful intersection of science and spirit.

TIPS FOR SUCCESSFUL CRYSTAL WORK

1. KNOW YOUR CRYSTALS

Figuring out which crystals carry specific energies that you need or want for your crystal work can seem like a daunting task. The list of options seems to be endless! Start small by choosing one or two crystals that you're drawn to and learn everything you can about them. Once you feel you understand your choices, add a couple more to learn about. As your list builds, keep logs of your collection.

2. KEEP TRACK

With the vast amount of options out there, it can be difficult to keep track of properties, uses, specific energies, solubility, and spellwork. Keeping logs or diaries of your crystals and their properties can offer a quick reference in times of need and help you keep inventory. It's also a good bird's-eye view of what you have so far and what you might want to add to the collection.

3. KNOW YOURSELF

One of the most important aspects of crystal work is knowing yourself. Not just who you are, what you wear, the music you like, or the foods you love. Knowing yourself means digging deep. You are a being made of energy, and crystals are too. You and your crystals have much to offer each other. But if you feel sad, for example, and only shove the feeling down instead of acknowledging and examining it, then the sadness goes unaddressed. And things that are left unaddressed tend to resurface in detrimental ways. Crystal energies can assist in addressing your emotions and thoughts, but you have to recognize what those are and their sources before calling in your crystal troops.

4. GET CREATIVE

Your inner-artist (yes, everyone has one) is strongly linked to your intuition. But sometimes the messages from your intuition can be hard to hear with all of the noise of our daily lives. One of the purest ways to dig deep and know yourself is to unleash your creative beast. Even if you don't consider yourself to be artistic, you actually are! Just the act of choosing a color coordinated outfit is a form of art. Flex your creativity muscles often to give yourself

an expressive outlet for the things buried deep within. This can take many forms: use a meditative coloring book, break out the canvas and brushes, take pictures of beautiful sights, treat yourself to some colored pencils or a fresh box of crayons, to name a few. Whatever your personal creative outlet might be, listen to the way it makes you feel, what your art might be telling you, and how your crystals can help.

5. CHECK YOUR VIBE

We are beings composed of a multitude of energies. These dictate our moods, our perceptions, and our communication. It's healthy to take a moment or two each day to check in with yourself. Stop and pinpoint your mood. Bad mood? What's making you grumpy? Feeling elated? What's making you so happy? Your crystals pick up on your energies so identify them, and if they are dragging you down, address them. Evaluate yourself from a place of love often.

6. RAISE YOUR VIBRATIONS

Crystals emit high energy vibrations, as do we. This is why we are drawn to them and their beauty! Daily life can make a lot of demands on our inner-selves. We are constantly bombarded with information—traffic lights, a manager's mood, that phone call you've been avoiding—and it becomes easy to be overwhelmed. The more that is piled on us, the lower our vibrations shrink until we react to the stress, typically in a negative way. In order to successfully connect with your crystals, you must rise to their vibrations. Do meditation and breathing exercises to soothe yourself and clear your cluttered mind.

7. SET INTENTIONS

Learning to set intentions is a powerful way to focus your crystal work. Let's say you feel it's time to find a romantic partner. You've reviewed your crystal logs and have decided that you need a rose quartz crystal to assist in some love spell work you're planning. As you set out to your favorite crystal vendor to find your stone, state your intention to your deity, your spirit, your guides, the universe or whomever you call on. It might go something like this, "Spirit (or your entity), my heart is open to finding my soul mate now. My intention is to find the exact rose quartz stone to assist me in finding love." Then once you get to the store, keep your intention in the forefront of your mind. This not only makes your desires clear for manifestation, but also activates your intuition. Setting intentions helps to focus the crystal energies to target the exact places you need them the most.

1

crystal selection, programming & preservation

While there are nearly 5,800 currently known naturally occurring mineral structures in the world, hundreds of new additions to that list are discovered annually. With this in mind, give yourself permission to not know every name or recognize compounds on sight. Disabuse yourself of the fantasy of having a complete collection. Our environment continues to evolve, and its chemical composition shifts with each industry we employ to keep our modern world spinning. Temperature, humidity, and even building and road construction in a given area all play a part in how these beloved treasures form. If nothing else, take comfort in knowing that when all else is unknowable, there is always a crystal forming somewhere just beneath the surface.

With so many options, purposes, and, of course, price points, how can you even begin to choose the stone that's right for you? When it comes to crystals and minerals, the investment you're making is an investment in a forever friend. Is it a pocket stone to keep with you for stressful days or for an energetic boost? An amulet to adorn you or to commemorate a moment in time? A statement piece for your home, or a powerful emblematic ornamentation to energize your business? This section will help you identify your needs, learn about the properties of a selection of more common crystals and how they correlate with your intentions, and some techniques for charging and maintaining their beauty.

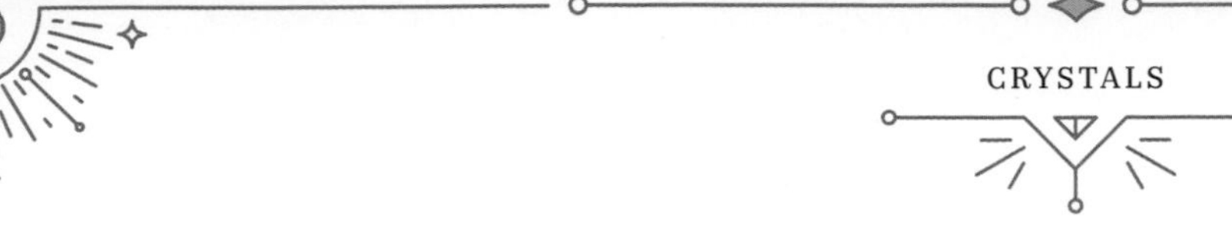

CRYSTAL SELECTION

With so many specimens in the world to choose from, you may wonder where you should begin. There is no correct answer to this, only what feels right for your personal practices. You may want to begin with your intentions. Are you looking for something to meditate with, or beautify your space? Are you purifying electromagnetic field (EMF) energy in your workspace, or hoping to protect your home from negative energy? Or maybe you're looking to amplify feelings of positivity and love. Each crystal has its own properties, as do their forms. While you may have a specific purpose in mind, it might be more appealing to choose intuitively. What are you most drawn to? Is it a specific type of stone or color? A carved form or a natural formation? What feelings does it invoke when you look at it? When you hold it?

Where and when you acquire your stones might influence your choice of which ones to take home with you. Since these specimens are of the earth, and formed over many years, availability and price are ever shifting. Overmining or political tumult can make it difficult to obtain pieces from particular areas. Since these pieces are energetically sensitive and influenced by both their surroundings and the people who mine and distribute them, it's worth noting where you source your collection from. Are prices too good to be true? Do a little research and see if you can confirm if they have been sustainably mined or part of a fair-trade program that provides some promise of protection to those who worked to unearth the precious crystals. Find out if they've been lab-treated or are in their natural condition. There are many guides available with details to help you spot a fake or altered specimen.

On the following pages, you'll find a list of specific crystal formations and their strengths. In the space provided, reflect on how each formation personally resonates with you. You might surprise yourself with the forms you are most drawn to versus those you had initially expected to seek out!

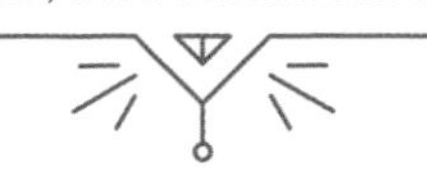

CLUSTER

Multiple points on a single base (matrix), fairly uniform in size. Many points help amplify power and are great to use as a base for charging smaller crystals.

Personal associations and intentions for use:

GENERATOR

Six-faceted, single terminated point, either alone or at center of matrix. Used to amplify and generate energy.

Personal associations and intentions for use:

ABUNDANCE

Generator or tower at the center of a matrix shared with cluster of smaller crystals at the base. Attracts abundance and wealth.

Personal associations and intentions for use:

DRUZY

Good for charging, relaxation, and promoting balance. Encourages ideas to come forward and wards off depression.

Personal associations and intentions for use:

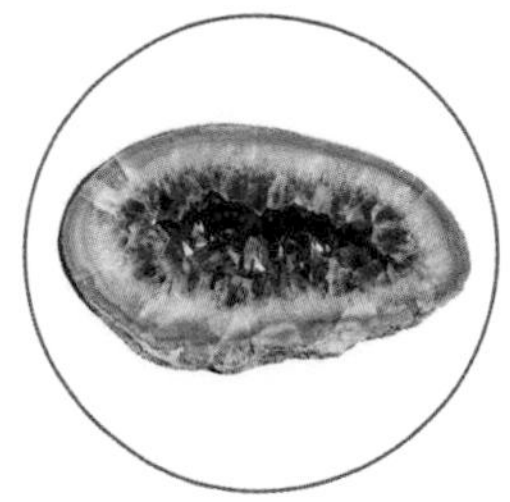

GEODE

Enclosed formation that works protectively, conserving, and then slowly releasing energy. Assists with grounding, internal healing, and decision-making.

Personal associations and intentions for use: ....

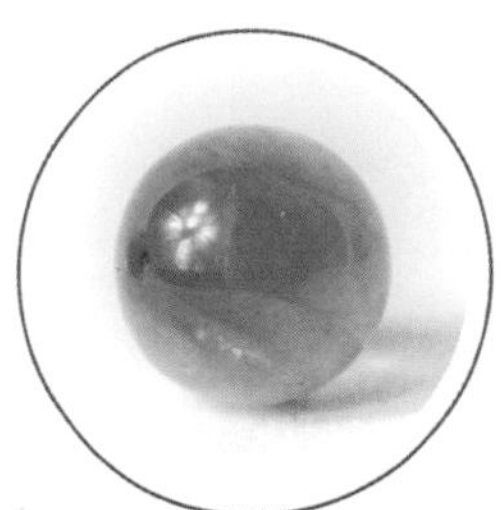

SPHERE

Radiates energy evenly and helps open the third eye. Used to create harmony and develop psychic powers.

Personal associations and intentions for use: ....

EGG

Used to amplify energies of fertility, and for new beginnings. Also said to provide healing and balance; often used for massage and acupressure.

Personal associations and intentions for use: ....

WORRY STONE/PALM STONE

Good for keeping with you at all times; helps quell worries and anxiety.

Personal associations and intentions for use: ....

PYRAMID

Powerful tool for manifestation; shape amplifies the properties of any stone. The square base provides grounding energy, the apex focuses your affirmations, the sides ward off negative vibrations and help clear blockages.

Personal associations and intentions for use:

SQUARE

Contained energy; highly grounding and easy to program.

Personal associations and intentions for use:

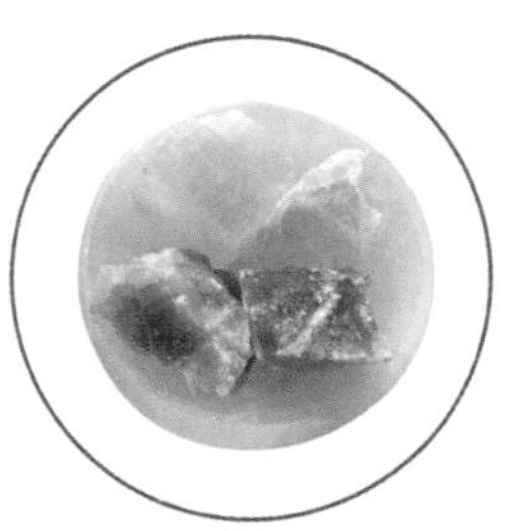

BOWL

Used for cleansing and charging other crystals and objects.

Personal associations and intentions for use:

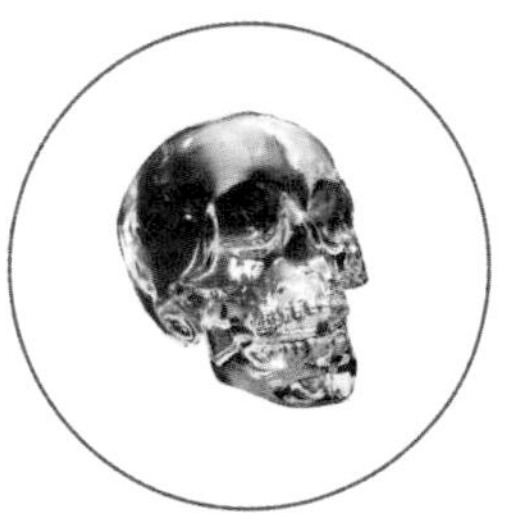

SKULL

Used to channel ancient knowledge and to connect with your guides and ancestors and your own higher intelligence. Also used to assist in breaking generational curses.

Personal associations and intentions for use:

HEART

Attracts feelings of love and amplifies positive energies. Increases fertility and soothes grief.

Personal associations and intentions for use: ______________________

____

____

AKASHIC LINES

Horizontal lines etched along the side of a crystal, said to hold multidimensional historical records. Great for meditation and looking into your deeper self.

Personal associations and intentions for use: ______________________

____

____

ISIS

Five-faceted with one large main face; used to amplify feminine energy. Encouraging, empowering, and uplifting.

Personal associations and intentions for use: ______________________

____

____

DOUBLE-TERMINATED

Points at both ends; absorbs and emits energy at the same time. Good for gridwork and removing blockages.

Personal associations and intentions for use: ______________________

____

____

TWIN

Two connected crystals (usually close in size) that share a base. Used to draw in soulmates of all sorts, balance yin and yang energy, and help solve relationship issues.

Personal associations and intentions for use:

RECORD KEEPER

Crystal with clearly etched pyramid shapes on at least one of its sides. Catalyst for growth and inner work.

Personal associations and intentions for use:

ENHYDRO AGATE

Water bubbles trapped inside the crystal growth. Helps utilize creative energy and emotion for manifestation.

Personal associations and intentions for use:

ELESTIAL

Inner planes, windows, and folds. Removes blockages and absorbs and transmutes negative energy.

Personal associations and intentions for use:

SCEPTER

Crystal formed around a rod; used to get to the core of problems.

Personal associations and intentions for use:

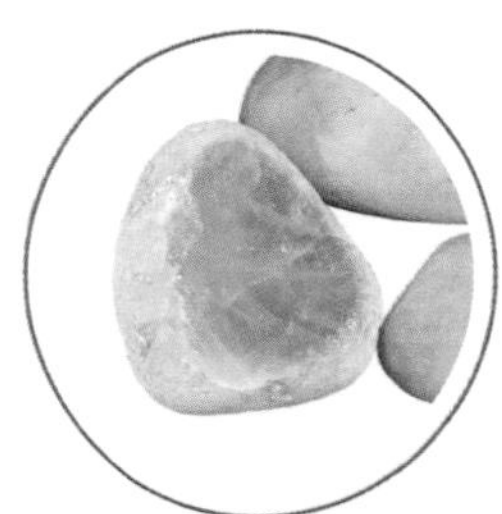

PICTURE WINDOW/SEER STONE

Sliced and polished on one side; used for scrying and during meditation.

Personal associations and intentions for use:

ANIMALS

Specific to individual and cultural associations. Generally used as a variety of worry stone.

Personal associations and intentions for use:

ANGELS

Used for connecting to guardian angels and spiritual work.

Personal associations and intentions for use:

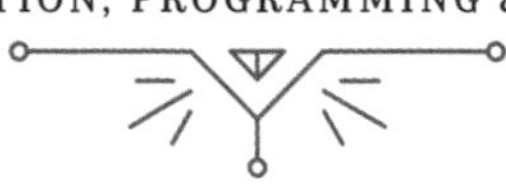

LEARN TO MEDITATE

This meditation is designed to teach you to clear your mind and connect with the powerful energies of crystals. Crystals hold very high vibrational energy, so in order to more deeply connect with them you must rise to their vibrational state. Adopting a regular meditation practice will help you raise your vibrations and stay in sync with your crystals but it also helps to center you and bring a calm state so that your intentions can be heard loud and clear, which is necessary for manifestation and spellwork. This meditation helps to connect you with the power of crystal shapes.

1. **Choose a shape that speaks to you in the areas of insight, inner work, and meditation. Use the previous list as a guide, but also listen closely to your intuition. You will feel drawn to the right stone and form, so go with it!**
2. **Prepare the space around you to bolster a sense of order and calm. When things are free of clutter and properly organized, our psyche can more easily relax and make space for insight. Clean up your space, put on some meditative music, lower the lights, light a candle—do what makes you feel a deep sense of inner peace.**
3. **Sit quietly on a chair, a pillow on the floor, on your bed, or wherever and however you feel most comfortable. You don't want to be distracted by aches and pains or an uncomfortable position.**
4. **Hold your chosen crystal formation in the palm of your hand and close your eyes.**
5. **Imagine your body full of dark, swirling smoke. Take long, cleansing breaths, breathing out the smoke, then breathing in a calming blue light, or whichever color your intuition signals you need to create a deep sense of inner peace. Blue always comes to mind as soothing for me, but maybe your personal color is a swirl of purple and gold, or a bright yellow, or a sage green. Colors are powerful conduits of energy, so allow yourself to imagine the color you need the most right now. As you breathe out the smoke, imagine it being replaced by your own loving energy color filling your body as you breathe in.**
6. **Once you feel centered, run your fingers all around the crystal, really feeling the shape. This is most effective with your eyes closed so you can focus on the physical sensation.**
7. **As you do this, visualize that everywhere your fingers run along the crystal a spark of energy is lighting the path across the surface of the shape. You are intermingling your energies with those of the crystal and its shape.**
8. **Hold the crystal in your palm and sit in quietude. Ask your deity, spirit, or your form of a spiritual guide to bring you insights about your self, the crystal work you plan to do, and the intentions you have for this work. You can also simply sit quietly without asking anything at all. Any message or insight that the universe has for you will come through as long as you're open. When you're done, take a deep breath.**

BREATHING EXERCISE

Now that you've read about the variety of crystal forms and learned to raise your vibrations, let's access your inventory of specific personal needs so you can get a sense of where crystals may be able to help you. Get comfortable, step away from the perma-scrolling, and listen to the backlog of inner voicemail you've been neglecting to check. A centering breathing exercise like this is great to do as a regular practice to open yourself to insight. Before you embark on crystal work, do a mediation or breathing exercise.

1. **To recenter yourself, close your eyes. Take long, thoughtful breaths. Try pranayama, or yogic breath-control techniques, to help you center your thoughts.**
2. **Slowly breathe in through your nose until your lungs and belly feel full, and then slowly breathe back out. As you breathe, keep your mouth closed and only use your nostrils.**
3. **Repeat this breathing pattern five full times or however many feel right for you.**
4. **Once you are ready, open your eyes and take three deep, cleansing breaths.**

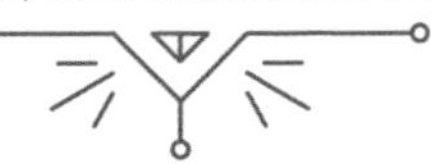

IDENTIFY AND PLAN

Now, reflect on your experience meditating and recentering. How do you physically feel? Do you feel lighter? What came up for you that needs to be addressed (think of that inner backlog of voicemail). Use the following prompts to dig deeper into your inner insight, identify problem areas, and a plan to address them.

1. **Problem area:** ....

   Crystal: ....

   Best formation to help: ....

2. **Problem area:** ....

   Crystal: ....

   Best formation to help: ....

3. **Problem area:** ....

   Crystal: ....

   Best formation to help: ....

4. **Problem area:** ....

   Crystal: ....

   Best formation to help: ....

5. **Problem area:** ....

   Crystal: ....

   Best formation to help: ....

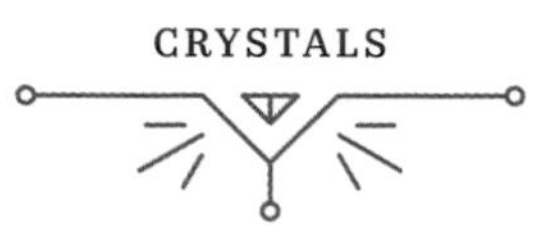

DIG DEEPER

How have you been feeling lately? When you are alone, what is the tone of your self-talk or internal dialogue?

When things are good, do you allow yourself a moment to savor that feeling? How do you honor your own efforts and accomplishments?

During a hectic day, how do you center yourself?

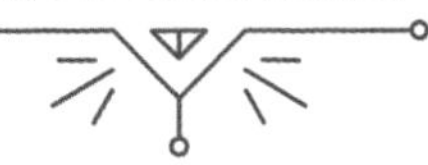

What brings you peace?

What environments or situations cause you stress?

When you are feeling mentally or emotionally drained, what helps energize you?

What short-term goals have you set for yourself recently?

What do you intend to accomplish in the long term?

What makes you feel like the best version of yourself?

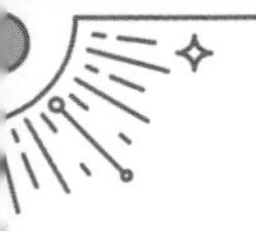
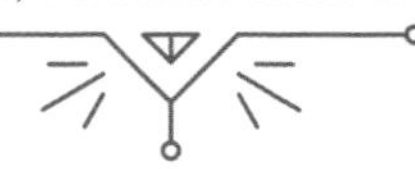

SPARK CREATIVITY

One of the best ways to address your needs is to tap into your own creativity. Think back on the meditation you just learned. Which colors came to you that invoked a sense of inner peace? Grab your markers, crayons, paint, or colored pencils and draw your own crystal formation. Fill your formation with your calming colors, add as many off-shoots as you like, create shapes within shapes, and layers upon layers. Let your intuition and creative soul guide you as you create. There is no right answer so you don't have to follow any rules—simply allow the inspiration to flow!

ENERGETIC INFLUENCES

Many crystals are traditionally associated with specific chakras, elements, and energies. But don't dismiss your responses to the journaling questions and personal experience. How you interact with and receive energy from various stones can be altered by everything from your astrological chart to your vibrational frequency. Those waves can shift frequently based on your emotional state, circles of concern and influence, and even media and content consumption. Just like you, crystals are affected by their environments, so a chunk of pyrite mined in Peru and kept archived for decades is likely to emit a different energy than a piece found in Italy in the 19th century, or even in the same cave in recent years. Stay open to your own perception and intuition, not just the word of any one crystal directory.

Refer to the list below for questions to ask yourself to help you diminish negative energetic influences. Then, I'll list some characteristics and categories to help you work on sorting through your personal associations with specific stones, as well as thoughts about the most common interpretations when looking to work with specific energy. As you encounter and learn more about individual properties of crystals and how they feel when you share physical space with them, list them to create a personalized inventory of crystal properties.

LOOK CLOSER

The following are some things to consider when understanding what might affect you and your crystals energetically. Ask yourself the following questions:

1. WHERE ARE MY VIBRATIONAL ENERGIES AT RIGHT NOW?

Crystals are packed full of vibrational energies that can deplete or replenish, as are you. Do a centering meditation or breathing exercise to clear internal space so you can see clearly which crystals you might need to you build up. Maybe you're lacking self-confidence, maybe you feel unlucky, or perhaps you can't shake sadness. Choose a crystal to fill your coffers. Alternately, choose crystals that can clear energies you don't want. Maybe you're seeing the world through a pessimistic lens, maybe you need to clear negativity, or perhaps you're overwhelmed and stressed. Truly listen to yourself and stay high vibrational with meditation and breathing exercises.

2. WHO IS INFLUENCING MY OUTLOOK AND ENERGY RIGHT NOW?

Who do you hang out with? Who do you live with? Who do you work with? Become clear on what energy influences they bring to your immediate life. Is your roommate always surly and standoffish? Are your friends judgmental or harsh with others? Are you out of sync with your coworkers? These energies can really impact your own and that of your crystals. This could be a great opportunity to set boundaries and use your crystals to shield you from negative influences.

3. WHAT MEDIA INFLUENCES DO I HAVE IN MY ENVIRONMENT?

What you choose to spiritually fill your environment with can have a significant impact on you, your psyche, your outlook, and your crystals. For example, some love a good true crime podcast but these can describe some pretty violent and devastating events. Stay balanced by mixing in podcasts that have a positive spin to give your empathy centers time to heal. Or maybe the music you listen to is a bit dark, the movies and television shows you watch more negative than uplifting, or the nightly news itself is creating anxiety. It's perfectly fine and natural to like these things but this spiritual environment can deplete positive energy, so create some balance with inspiring podcasts, shows, and music to lighten the atmosphere.

4. DO I NEED TO START LIMITING MY SCREENTIME?

Are you being kind to yourself with the amount of social media you're exposing yourself to? While social media has many benefits—keeping up with friends and family, memes that bring laughter, a break from boredom—it can also have a detrimental impact on how you see yourself and your accomplishments. It's possible that you have felt compelled to compare yourself with others, have become unsatisfied with your healthy, hardworking body, or feel the need to "keep up with the Joneses" by buying new things. These energies have a negative impact on you internally and, in turn, your crystals. Try limiting your social media time and see how your outlook changes.

5. WHERE WAS MY CRYSTAL SOURCED?

Not all crystals are kindly harvested from their sources. But unless you can track down the country of origin and the actual mine it came from, it can be difficult to find out if your stone was ethically sourced. Build a relationship with your crystal vendor. Ask important questions like what the source of their merchandise is and if the workers are treated fairly. Also, don't opt for the cheapest option. Sure, there are good deals out there, but if you find a crystal that is vastly cheaper than others like it on the market, this is usually a red flag that there were some corners cut while sourcing, or that it's a counterfeit. To be surest, just source your own! There are many crystal mines in the United States where you can venture in and find your own treasures. Always research as much as you can in order to avoid unethical choices and ensure the energies are positive and kind.

MY CRYSTAL ASSOCIATIONS

Keeping in mind what you've learned so far about both crystals and yourself, write in which crystals you believe will help you with each situation. Continue to add to this list as your knowledge grows.

Grounding:

Energizing:

Protection/safety:

Energetic reset/cleansing:

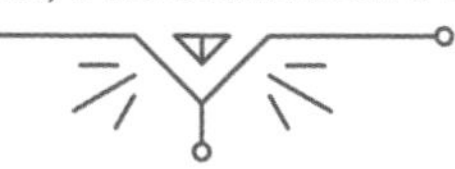

Enhancing creativity:

Manifesting love:

Lucid dreaming/dream recall:

Sexual energy/fertility:

Prosperity/abundance:

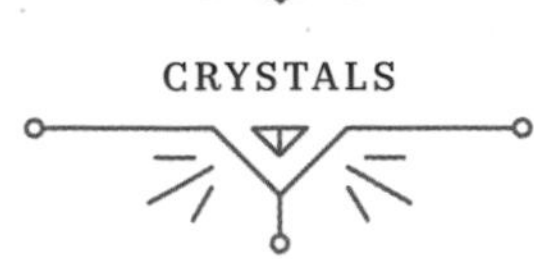

CRYSTAL CARE AND ENERGETIC MAINTENANCE

In the words of our fellow lover of crystals, Nikola Tesla, "If you want to find the secrets of the universe, think in terms of energy, frequency and vibration." Each of the stones in your collection has its own energy and attributed powers, and, just like us, sometimes that energy is drained from overexertion. To replenish your crystals, you must cleanse, rest, and recharge them. But what does that look like?

Incense and other smudging herbs are a great way to replenish your pieces, as well as your surroundings and personal energy. White sage is popular but is currently considered an at-risk species, meaning it has been overharvested and is approaching endangerment, so be mindful of effective alternatives. If you feel you must use white sage, purchase it from the Indigenous communities that have traditionally utilized and maintained it. There is a bounty of other herbs, wood, incense, and flowers that are nontoxic and accessible for your needs. Lavender, rosemary, various mints, wormwood, cedar, rosebud, and sweetgrass all work for energy clearing, and they smell lovely. Frankincense, myrrh, copal, and dragon's blood have been used for centuries to sanctify spaces, and a little goes a very long way. The smoke from burning any of these materials can be used to cleanse your space as a whole or by passing pieces through the plumes. As always, be mindful of fire safety, use appropriate vessels, and never leave an active burn unattended. Also, remember to clear your space of smoke after you have consecrated and cleansed your intended objects and area. You're working toward clearing energy, so leaving them hanging in the air won't help you get them out the door. Literally. Crack a window; let some fresh air in and the old energy out.

Salt water is also a great way to cleanse your crystals. That can mean submerging them for a few hours or days or putting them in natural saltwater. Be mindful of what each material needs and can withstand. Selenite, the powerhouse of energy cleansers, will brittle and break in water—a painful lesson that's better not learned firsthand. A good rule of thumb is that most crystals whose names end in 'ite' tend to be water-soluble. That means double-check all of your malachite, fluorite, sodalite, and so forth for their solubility and your peace of mind. Most common stones, hard crystals, and tumbles are safe for short periods of time in water. Avoid submerging brittle, porous, or rust-prone materials. Sorry, pyrite, no tub time for you! Sprinkling consecrated water on areas where you keep your collection is also a good technique. We'll get into a few water-charging techniques later.

Using light to cleanse and charge crystals is a great option. Take those beauties out in the sun or under the moonlight and let the light shine on them! This should be safe with most of your stones, though more vibrantly colored crystals can fade from direct sun.

Burying your stones is said to help return them to their source energy. If you have access to an undisturbed spot, you only need to bury them a few inches down to ensure they are covered. Let them be for anywhere from a day to a week. But don't forget to X mark the spot! No need to tear your garden up in the process—brown rice will work similarly. Bury your piece beneath the grains in a bowl or other vessel, and leave them for 24 hours. Once you've retrieved your pieces, dispose of the rice. You don't want to ingest the energies you thoughtfully purged from your crystals.

Sound cleansing is another method that can be done with ease. You can achieve this with a meditation singing bowl, tuning fork, bell, or even chanting. This is a great option for a big collection, for individual pieces, or if you are concerned about exposure to elements. Find the tone that feels right to you, and make sure that it is loud enough for the vibration to encompass your desired space.

CLEANSING DIARY

Now that we've discussed some of your cleansing options, take stock of what works best for you and your needs. Use the following pages to log dates, moon phases, and even events that made you feel like it was time to cleanse your crystals. You can do this regularly in a dedicated crystal diary, and refer back to it to remind you of how each of your crystals tells you it's time for a bath.

Crystal: ....

Date: ....

Moon phase/event: ....

Method of cleanse: ....

✦

Crystal: ....

Date: ....

Moon phase/event: ....

Method of cleanse: ....

✦

Crystal: ....

Date: ....

Moon phase/event: ....

Method of cleanse: ....

✦

Crystal: ....

Date: ....

Moon phase/event: ....

Method of cleanse: ....

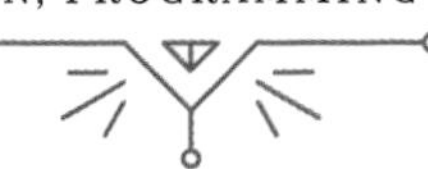

Crystal:

Date:

Moon phase/event:

Method of cleanse:

Crystal:

Date:

Moon phase/event:

Method of cleanse:

Crystal:

Date:

Moon phase/event:

Method of cleanse:

Crystal:

Date:

Moon phase/event:

Method of cleanse:

Crystal:

Date:

Moon phase/event:

Method of cleanse:

CLEANSING TOOLKIT INVENTORY

It's easy to lose track of supplies and either overstock or realize the coffers have been depleted during the last energy reset. Use the space below to log your cleansing inventory, suppliers, the cleansing tools you've had success with, and what types of energy they clear (e.g., blocked energy, negative energy, self-doubt, and so forth). Describing the scent can be helpful for quick reference. Maybe someone who lives in your home reacts poorly to the smell of sandalwood incense, or you're cleansing your office so you want something scent-free. Refer to this when it's time to restock.

Cleansing tool: ....

Energy it clears: ....

Source: ....

Frequency of use: ....

Description of scent: ....

✦

Cleansing tool: ....

Energy it clears: ....

Source: ....

Frequency of use: ....

Description of scent: ....

✦

Cleansing tool: ....

Energy it clears: ....

Source: ....

Frequency of use: ....

Description of scent: ....

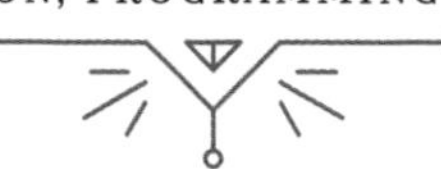

Cleansing tool: ....

Energy it clears: ....

Source: ....

Frequency of use: ....

Description of scent: ....

Cleansing tool: ....

Energy it clears: ....

Source: ....

Frequency of use: ....

Description of scent: ....

Cleansing tool: ....

Energy it clears: ....

Source: ....

Frequency of use: ....

Description of scent: ....

Cleansing tool: ....

Energy it clears: ....

Source: ....

Frequency of use: ....

Description of scent: ....

PROGRAMMING

Programming your crystal means to fill it with intention—your hopes for prosperity, progress, protection, love, and all the positive energy that you seek to draw into your energy field. These may seem like hefty aspirations, and they are, but they're also basic desires of the human condition. As many facets as your crystals have, so has your life.

Each crystal and mineral possesses its own energy and power. Consider its properties and your specific needs when choosing which crystal to utilize in helping you attain your goals. To program your piece, you must be perfectly clear on what you need from it.

STEP 1

Before you begin, do a mediation or breathing exercise, then think on which crystal you connect with the most when considering your goals. Which feels like it brings your most desired attributes? Which feels like it's meant to clear you of negative thoughts and energy? What is your intuition telling you? Choose your crystal based on your answers.

STEP 2

To program your piece, you must be perfectly clear on what you need.

STEP 3

Hold your crystal in your hands, close your eyes, and make your mind still. Feel your hands warming the crystal, infusing your energy with its own.

STEP 4

Envision your goals, going into great detail. Then, envision which powers within the crystal that you'd like to activate. They can appear as colors, different types of light, or as symbolic manifestations.

STEP 5

Hold the crystal to your mouth so that it is enveloped in your breath. Speak or whisper your intentions into the crystal.

TIPS FOR SETTING INTENTIONS

The most effective way to program your crystals is to be clear about what you're asking them to do. For many, setting intentions is unchartered territory. Here are some tips for setting intentions.

* **Think about what you really want or need. Do you need luck on your side at a job interview? Are you seeking protection from negative forces? Get very specific. You must be clear with what you seek.**
* **Chances are, there are some subconscious blockages that are preventing you from being clear on your goals. Do a meditation or breathing exercise to clear some mental clutter, then try to identify what is blocking you. What is the true source of your bad mood? What is specifically causing you anxiety? Find solutions for things that you can change, and work toward releasing things you can't do anything about. Then, return to your programming.**
* **A mantra is an effective form of intention on a large scale, usually relating to your life as a whole. When you create a mantra, you have narrowed down exactly what will make you happy and whole, and you use the phrase as a reminder of what that looks like for you. Think of an intention as a "mantra for the moment."**
* **Ask for what you want, but don't try to control the outcome. The universe, or your personal form of spiritual guide, is seeing your life from a high-vibrational state and knows exactly what you truly need. Your intention might be for good luck during a job interview, but perhaps your spiritual guide knows something you don't. Maybe that workplace looks great from the outside looking in but behind the scenes there is a toxic environment that will hurt you more than serve you. Ask for what you need, but be open to all outcomes.**
* **Turn any question into a statement. Rather than ask, "Can I have good luck for this interview?" try stating it outright. This helps to tune into and manifest your goals. Turn your questions into positive affirmations: "My intention is that I will have good luck and a successful interview."**
* **Be reasonable about your intentions. Not all intentions have to meet a lofty goal. They're great for big purposes but they also serve smaller purposes as well. You might just need something universal like, "My intention is that I will have gratitude today for all that I have." If you want to program your crystals and you don't have a need or want in mind, it's also effective to be broader with something like, "I dedicate the energies of this crystal to positive outcomes in my life."**

PROGRAMMING LOG

Use the following log to keep track of which crystals worked for a specific situation after programming. You can continue this log in the back of this book or in a dedicated crystal journal, referring back whenever a situation arises where you need to address a specific issue.

Date:

Intentions and goals:

Crystal utilized:

Date:

Intentions and goals:

Crystal utilized:

Date:

Intentions and goals:

Crystal utilized:

Date:

Intentions and goals:

Crystal utilized:

Date:

Intentions and goals:

Crystal utilized:

Date:

Intentions and goals:

Crystal utilized:

Date:

Intentions and goals:

Crystal utilized:

Date:

Intentions and goals:

Crystal utilized:

Date:

Intentions and goals:

Crystal utilized:

PRESERVATION

You've grown your collection, and you've invested in each piece with intent and affection. By now, you have come to love specific things about their forms, how they feel in your hands, and the way the light catches at certain angles. You keep your little friends dust-free, cleansed, and charged. The last thing you would ever want is for them to be harmed in any way. But life has a way of testing intentions against realities, and sometimes, our perfectly imperfect crystal friends are nudged further into the realm of flawed or damaged —your fluorite faded because you left it in direct sun for too long; your selenite charging slab inadvertently served as a guest's drink coaster and has taken on too much moisture and cracked; or the most painful of all, your favorite beautiful glistening cluster slipped off its perch or out of your hands and broke into countless shards.

None of these scenarios is ideal, but try to remember that, no matter what their physical form is, these pieces have not lost any of their energy. You can still utilize them as pocket stones or place them around your home or workspace. You can integrate them into your garden, create protective satchels or jewelry, and use them to infuse moonwater and a variety of potions or to embellish something cherished.

Always take a moment to honor the form of your damaged crystals. Thank them for their assistance in your various practices and for beautifying your life. Write down how the damage occurred so that you can avoid repeating your mistake and how you will repurpose the crystal with new intentions. This isn't for the crystal; this is for you to reflect on the fact that energy can't be destroyed, only shifted.

REPURPOSE AND REUSE

When the leaves of a beautiful tree turn colors in the fall, the tree is no less lovely for this transformation. In fact, it may be all the more stunning because of it! This is how damaged crystals work. They might have a crack or have been broken, but they still hold powerful energies that can be used to your advantage. One way to repurpose your damaged crystals is to make a cleansing spray. A cleansing spray can be used to cleanse a room, your tools, your altar, or anywhere that you feel an energetic reset needs to happen. This is an ethical alternative to using white sage or palo santo wood. There are many ways to make a spray so use these instructions as a general guide and try creating your own.

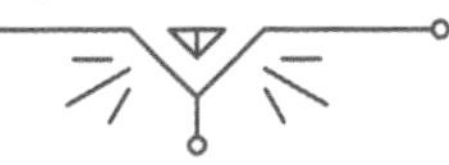

✧✧✧

* Obtain a small spray bottle (approximately 4 ounces, or 120 ml). I suggest you use one with colored glass because UV light can interfere with some essential oils.
* Create a cleansing essential oil blend. There are many oils that have cleansing properties like lavender, sandlewood, rosemary, or tea tree. Get creative!
* Choose a solubilizer. This is an ingredient that helps to emulsify the oil and vodka or distilled water so that you have an even distribution of oil throughout your mixture. It's inexpensive and can be found online at most major retailers or with your essential oil vendor.
* Select your non-water-soluble damaged crystals.
* If using distilled water or moonwater, choose a natural preservative. In order to avoid a mold infestation or bacterial growth, you can add a store-bought preservative, but for this purpose we will use vodka as our base liquid, as it dissipates quickly, doesn't stain, and naturally repels bacteria. To fill your 4-ounce bottle, you'll need at least 1/2 cup (120 ml) of vodka or Everclear.

STEP 1

Begin by adding your essential oil or blend to your desired strength of scent and the number of drops of solubilizer that the brand you have recommends for 4-ounce mixtures. This should be labeled either on the bottle or the instruction sheet it comes with.

STEP 2

Add your damaged crystals or crystal shards.

STEP 3

Fill the bottle the rest of the way with vodka and gently shake to mix.

STEP 4

From here, set an intention for your spray. Hold it in your hands and state out loud what you need from the spray. Your intention might look something like, "My intention is that this spray will cleanse the spaces I inhabit from negative energies and influences." Let it come from your heart.

DAMAGED CRYSTAL TRANSFORMATION LOG

Date:

Crystal:

How the damage happened:

New intention/use:

Date:

Crystal:

How the damage happened:

New intention/use:

Date:

Crystal:

How the damage happened:

New intention/use:

Date:

Crystal:

How the damage happened:

New intention/use:

Date:

Crystal:

How the damage happened:

New intention/use:

Date:

Crystal:

How the damage happened:

New intention/use:

Date:

Crystal:

How the damage happened:

New intention/use:

Date:

Crystal:

How the damage happened:

New intention/use:

MOONWATER

Water is a powerful energy conduit and, in conjunction with the ever-potent moon, can create a magical elixir or cleansing potion to add to your spiritual arsenal. It can be used to cleanse your crystals and tools, to sprinkle about an energetically corrupted space, to infuse into a magical bath, or to drink with tea. While the full moon is considered to be the most powerful phase during which to charge your water (or crystals, for that matter), all phases have their associated properties and strengths. Many say that the only time you should avoid tapping into lunar energies is during an eclipse. Lunar eclipses are considered times for release and reset, not for harnessing energy, since they are said to reveal our shadows and darkest energy. Each full moon holds its own specific energy, depending on what time of year it occurs and its astrological placement. When utilizing crystals in tandem with moonwater, you should always be mindful of which are water safe to avoid splintering or corrosion. If you intend on ingesting the water and have infused it with crystals, make sure that they are non-toxic and skin-safe. Do your research, please! There's nothing magical about needing to contact Poison Control. You can easily avoid this by using an indirect method of infusion: Place your chosen crystals on top of or beside your water vessel while charging. Always be intentional when choosing a moon phase during which to charge your moonwater and crystals.

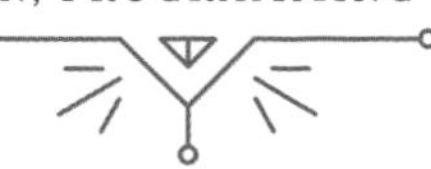

MOON PHASES

NEW MOON

Good for setting intentions, manifestations, new beginnings, and cleansing purposes.

WAXING MOON

Growth, planning, new projects, and taking action.

FULL MOON

Power, success, bringing goals into fruition, and assisting in charging items.

WANING MOON

Release, banishing, self-reflecting, and letting go.

MAKING MOONWATER

Follow the instructions below any time you need to make moonwater.

STEP 1

Choose your vessel and fill it with water. It's good to have a container that matches your intentions, be it a simple glass jar or bottle, or something ornate and embellished. Fresh natural sources of water are best: rainwater, spring water, river water, and so forth. If you plan on drinking it, make sure it is safe and clean.

STEP 2

Find a spot that gets direct moonlight: Windowsills, patios, a secure spot somewhere outside. Use whatever is accessible and allows your vessel to absorb the most light.

STEP 3

Set your intentions. Speak them, write them down and place them beneath your vessel or tape them to the side, meditate over the water, say a prayer; do whatever works for you. When you are satisfied and your intuition alerts you, your water has been infused with said intentions.

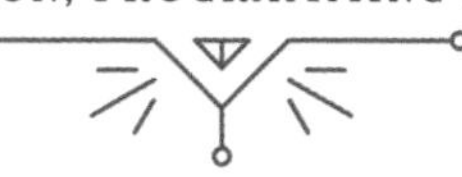

STEP 4

Choose a stone that suits your intentions. Place your crystal on top of or beside your vessel (if nontoxic and safe for consumption, you may place the crystal within). Make sure you have a lid that snugly seals. You may also choose to infuse your water with other magical elements, such as botanicals and herbs, which also carry significant amounts of magical properties. Always be mindful of the toxicity level of the elements you use, and be knowledgeable about their edibility and potential contact risks. Again, research, research, research. Knowledge is power.

STEP 5

Leave your vessel overnight in the moonlight to charge. In the morning, it will be ready to use however you see fit. If you're seeking a stronger infusion, leave it out for one full moon cycle.

CRYSTALS FOR YOUR PLANTS

As previously mentioned, a great way to cleanse your crystals is to set them out in your garden or bury them for a brief period in order to help them ground and reconnect with their source. But it's also worth noting that there are many stones that are believed to boost your garden's fertility and maintain health. This isn't limited to outdoor spaces, as they can be highly beneficial to houseplants. They not only beautify planters and ward off pests, their energies promote growth and lower stress vibrations. This is a good opportunity to repurpose damaged crystals!

Each garden, planter, and pot is a new chance to delight yourself: Beautify your plants and planters, promote health and growth, foster peace for your plants in a hectic environment, or create a fairy garden.

Refer to this list of crystals that are great for plants and gardens to get you started. Feel free to add your favorites. Always remember to research and check specific properties of the crystals you are utilizing. Water solubility and corrosion are real, so save yourself the heartache of further damaging crystals and potentially compromising your soil. Never forget to cleanse your crystals before use, even if they'll be nestled in dirt.

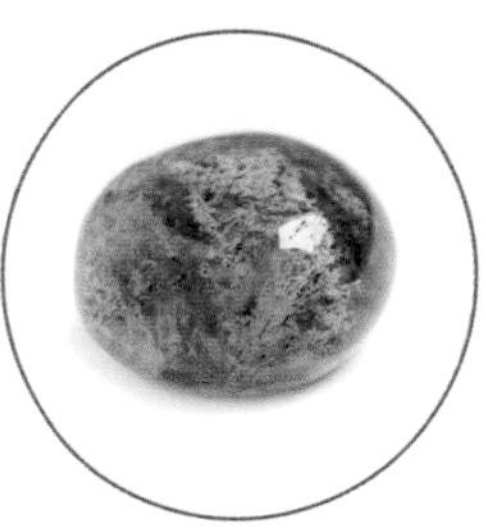

MOSS AGATE

Moss agate is casually known as "the gardener's stone," making it an obvious choice for incorporating among your plant friends. It is said to strengthen your connection to your garden and to revitalize energy, whether it's you or the plant leaves that are feeling a bit wilted. Promotes health and vitality in your plants and provides confidence to those of us struggling to activate the green in our thumbs.

CLEAR QUARTZ

The multipurpose star of your crystal arsenal, clear quartz is always ready to amplify and be programmed to suit your purposes in the garden as readily as in all other applications. This all-purpose crystal stimulates growth, promotes healing, and reflects light, casting rainbows in the process.

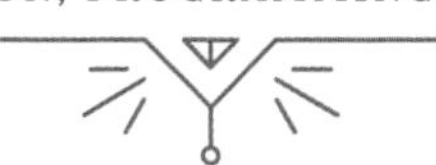
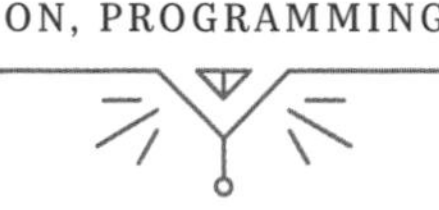

AMETHYST

Often dubbed as one of the master healers, amethyst brings a soothing energy to your garden and provides a protective energy to ailing plants. Promotes feelings of tranquility along with spiritual connection.

GREEN AVENTURINE

Great for new plantings, this crystal helps absorb negative energy, which is most useful to reduce transplant shock when repotting or planting new blooms. Considered to be a stone of great luck, it attracts new opportunities and encourages optimistic energy, promoting growth. Perfect for cuttings and seedlings alike.

TIGER'S EYE

Tiger's eye is a powerful tool for grounding and warding off negative energy. Best used to encourage root growth and assist struggling plants, protecting them from destructive energy. Said to bring about abundance in the garden.

GREEN CALCITE

Said to promote healing and plant growth, this stone is closely related to the heart chakra, so its energy is great for stressed plants (and their humans). Popular for its ability to remove energy blocks.

CREATE A FAIRY GARDEN

Fairies grace our gardens with mischief and flights of fancy while also helping plants bloom and grow. Follow the below instructions to set up your own fairy garden to let them know that this is an attractive place to make a home. Gather together the items on the following page, and mark their placement in your plan. If you can't access a certain item, simply close your eyes, conjure up images of the fairies that you'd like to attract, and use your intuition to choose a replacement item.

Draw a basic sketch of your garden layout, then mark the places where each item will live. Refer back to this sketch to remember where you have placed your crystals.

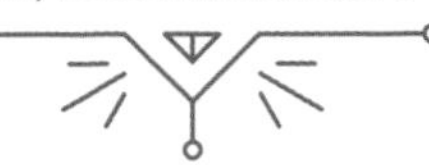

Use this list to choose items and which crystals you'd like to incorporate into your fairy garden, then sketch out their placement on your garden map.

* **Acorns: Fairies recharge their energy from oak trees. Acorns will let them know they can recharge in your garden.**
* **Windchimes: They love music and will be attracted to the tinkling notes. You can use metal or glass chimes, or make your own from a selection of fairy crystals.**
* **Foxglove plants: Very popular with fairies, they use these blooms in fashion and fairy magic, and they admire their beauty. Foxglove will also attract hummingbirds, fierce allies of fairies.**
* **Honey: Just a small bowlful or capful. Fairies have a ferocious sweet tooth! While they'll be happy with any type of sweet treat, they prefer natural golden honey. Be sure to change this regularly to avoid attracting pests.**
* **Clear quartz: This is a must for the garden. Place it somewhere prominent, as it naturally attracts light and happiness. Fairies are strongly attracted to this stone. Be mindful of the formation of the crystal you choose! My fairy altar has a clear quartz carved heart, as I want to attract love.**
* **Calcite: Fairy stones to attract good luck and protection from the fairies.**
* **Aquamarine: For insight and foresight.**

2

the energetic purposes of crystals

There are a variety of ways to approach using stones to influence and alter the energy in your personal space. While I'm not talking about formal energy work like Reiki, Ayurvedic practices, First Nation traditions, or even Western esoteric or Pagan techniques, I will touch upon approaches used by many of these groups throughout this chapter. Crystal healing and humans harnessing the energy from it have been documented as early as 4500 BC, when the ancient Sumerians integrated them into their formulas. A further geographic reach, around 400 BC, is noted in early astrological studies written in Sanskrit, as well as being frequently linked to Atlantean mythology by Plato. There is much information to mine.

All things in this universe hold their own energetic frequencies and EMFs, crystals not least of them. Crystals hold vast amounts of vibrational energy as well as acting as amplifiers, invigorating preexisting energy and boosting the energy of other crystals. Clear quartz, labradorite, moonstone, amethyst, and fluorite are the most common examples, all serving as boosters. These can be used in tandem with other crystals to amplify energies while purifying your space of negativity, attracting love, conjuring luck and calling for protection, or to neutralize and reset another crystal, yourself, or a room.

In the following chapter, you will learn to identify amplifiers and methods to achieve your intentions through harnessing crystal magic with spellwork, employing classic grid formations, correlating with chakra fields, and even employing a freestyle formation of your own to match your intention and mood.

ENERGETIC AMPLIFIERS

We all need an extra boost sometimes: An energetic amplifier to tune up our intuition, energize our intentions, and generally raise the volume on that inner voice that narrates the positive mental attitude that gets us through our days. When things have become overwhelming and you need to boost the properties of your crystals, turn to this list to get you started.

CLEAR QUARTZ

The multipurpose powerhouse of any collection, this stone is strong enough to energize you on its own, clearing your chakras of negative energy. It's also versatile, lending that same energy to assist in amplifying the powers of other crystals you team it up with.

Utilize: Put the clear quartz in your nondominant hand, on jewelry, or in a sachet, or place it on your altar to add clarity and power to any spell, promote deep soul healing, and enhance psychic abilities.

CARNELIAN

Carnelian is known as a strong motivator and igniter of creative passion. This stone will help inspire you when you're feeling blocked by procrastination and fear. Said to spark sexual energy, confidence, and self-empowerment.

Utilize: When you're feeling particularly insecure, creatively blocked, or unmotivated, place this in your pocket or purse and rub the stone each time these feelings rear their heads. If someone you love is experiencing these things, place one crystal to the right of that person's front doorway to invite in self-love and creativity. You can also do this at your own front door.

CITRINE

Another stone of powerful motivation, and said to harness solar energy, it will help you achieve an optimistic outlook and push away negativity. Works to inspire you in your endeavors while shielding you from any negativity others may project in your direction.

Utilize: Place the citrine either somewhere safe outside or on your windowsill, where it can absorb the warmth and light of the sun. After two hours of basking the stone in light, place it on your root chakra and do a meditation of the stone becoming warmer and brighter over time. Imagine that light radiating into each area of your body, particularly your chakras.

ORANGE CALCITE

Works to shift feelings of heaviness in spirit and body. Promotes vitality and a general feeling of lightheartedness to encourage the release of negative habits and perspectives.

Utilize: To lift heaviness, clear negativity, and promote sharp focus, light an orange candle that has been anointed with olive oil. Place the orange calcite near the candle so that it is kissed by the soft light. Think of an affirmation that is specific to you and your situation, for example, *As negativity lifts and dissipates, I am light, clear-minded, and energetic*. Repeat this out loud three times, then let the candle burn out.

GARNET

Boosts self-confidence and reignites passion. Stimulates libido and strengthens physical and sexual bonds.

Utilize: When you're feeling the pressure of loneliness and want to attract a partner, or you need to reignite an existing spark, gather together a small handful of garnet chips. Place a sprinkling in the corners of your bedroom, then place the remaining chips in a sachet beneath your pillow. As you do, repeat the phrase, *Garnet, I call on you; Passion, I harness you; Goddess Venus, I implore you to ignite burning love*.

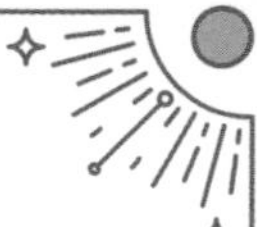

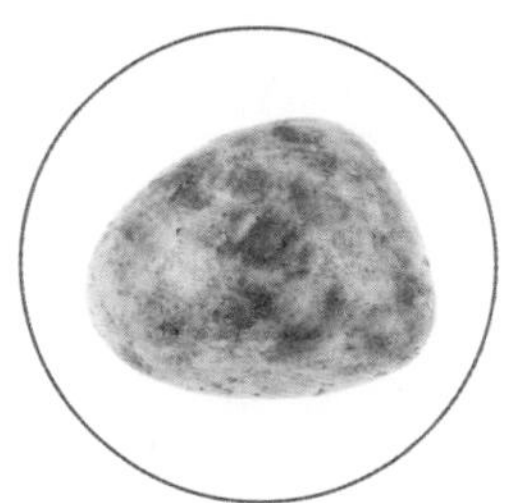

SUNSTONE

Strengthens intuition and confidence, and encourages feelings of independence and self-sufficiency. Promotes luck, enthusiasm, and an attitude of benevolence.

Utilize: If you're feeling in need of confidence, luck, and success, begin by bathing the stone in moonwater or a sunlight bath to promote balance. Once cleansed and balanced, place it anywhere near your body. You can sew some chips into a seam in your clothing, place a stone in your pocket, or wear it on jewelry; the important part is that it is near your physical body so that it can radiate its vibrations into your own energy and infuse into your aura.

TIGER'S EYE

Amplifies inner strength, courage, and ambition. Inspires willpower, a sense of purpose, and mental clarity, while stabilizing and grounding moods. Said to boost psychic abilities.

Utilize: This stone is great for help with a job interview, when meeting new people, if you're nervous about an event, or you have to face a tough situation. In these times, hold a cleansed tiger's eye in your hand to warm it and fuse its energy with your own. Then, place it over your heart and say aloud three times, *I am courageous, I am strong, I am powerful*. Carry the stone with you.

VIBE CHECK

When using energetic amplifiers, it's important that you have clear focus on which specific energies you need to give a boost to. Think about where you are in this moment emotionally and spiritually, then answer the following questions to hone your focus.

1. **Sometimes certain feelings can weigh us down and prevent us from doing the things we want to do to accomplish our goals. What feels like a weight around your neck lately? Have feelings of anxiety been bogging you down? Are you insecure about something? Write it out.**

2. **What energies do you currently feel are holding you up? What feelings of strength do you currently possess?**

3. **Looking at the qualities that are lifting you up, choose some crystals from the energetic amplifiers crystal list that will boost the positive feelings that you do have. Which crystals are right for you right now?**

4. **In what ways can you use your chosen crystals to balance your energies?**

PURIFIERS AND PROTECTORS

No one is able to completely avoid having negativity enter their physical and emotional space. Our moods are affected by environment, ailments, interactions with other humans, and even subconscious anxieties. Seeking balance, clearing out energetic disturbances, and attempting to reset to a neutral atmosphere are natural impulses when things feel askew. Refer to this list for a quick reference of stones and uses that could assist you in purifying your space, aura, EMFs,—and even other stones.

BLACK TOURMALINE

Considered one of most powerful protective crystals for removing blockages, clearing the aura, and shielding against and absorbing negative energy. Takes what it absorbs and turns it into positive grounded energy.

Utilize: This is a "catchall" stone, so to repel negative energies, start by cleansing your space with incense or sprinkling saltwater (use a sprig of rosemary as a dipping wand). Place a black tourmaline stone beside each doorway and window to block negative energy from entering and keep positive energy in.

SHUNGITE

Mineraloid long thought to possess strong purification abilities, even being used by soldiers to purify their water. Cleanses the aura, activates all seven chakras, and detoxifies negativity of the body and mind. Grounds emotions, and is known to block the output of excess radiation.

Utilize: To block electromagnetic energy and repel radiation, place one shungite stone near each of your electronic devices.

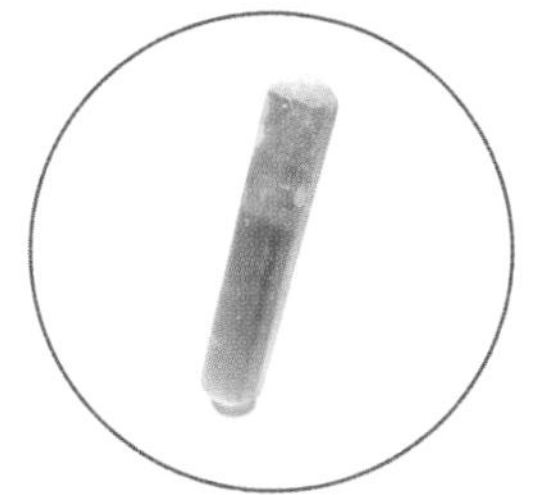

SELENITE

High-vibration purifier and spiritual healer often referred to as "liquid light" because it embodies the essence of pure light. Cleanses away negativity, and pushes stagnant blockages out, allowing for the positive flow of calm and clear thoughts and emotions. A valuable addition to your collection, being known as a protective shield of your person and environment, an elevator of intuitive abilities, and a faithful assistant in charging and magnifying the powers of all stones it interacts with.

Utilize: In times of need, cleanse your selenite by placing it under the light of the next full moon, and leave it overnight. Place it directly on your spine for at least 15 minutes. This will infuse your backbone with grounding, healing, energetic light.

AMETHYST

The "all-healer," working positively on plants, animals, and humans alike. Promotes growth, and counteracts negativity with pure, loving energy to balance out bad habits and negative thought patterns. Guards against psychic attack, while also soothing hot tempers, and calming anxiety.

Utilize: When you're so upset that you can think of little else and you feel yourself being worked into a frenzy, place a cleansed amethyst in each pocket, wear it as jewelry, or place it in each room in your home. Then, make a cup of your favorite tea and place a stone at the bottom of the cup and sip. As the tea warms you, the amethyst protects you.

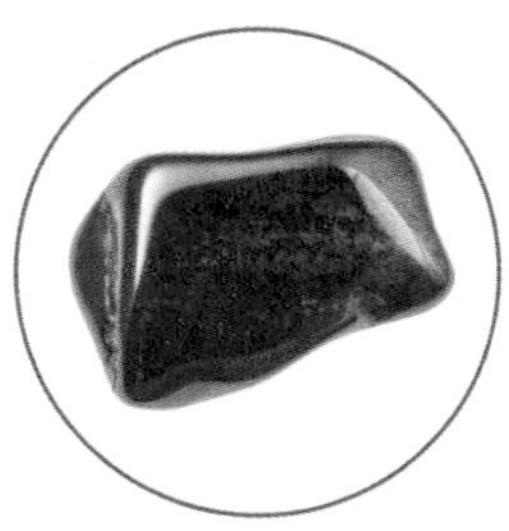

BLOODSTONE

Calms the mind, and alleviates aggressive and impatient energy. As its name denotes, strongly linked with heart chakra, said to aid in circulation and purification of the blood. Protects from harmful EMFs emitted by electronic devices. Known to stimulate vivid dreams and revitalize energy.

Utilize: When that paycheck hasn't cleared yet, your partner is frustrating you, or you need something done quickly but have little time, feelings of agitation can rise, blocking your calm nature and making you think negative thoughts. When you feel that pressure mounting, hold a bloodstone to your heart, and chant three times: *I am calm, I am at peace, all things work out when it is their time.*

OBSIDIAN

A powerful mineraloid, absorbing negativity, and working as an intense psychic shield. Tool for deep healing, said to assist in the release of outdated behaviors and perceptions, and the dissolution of stress. Lends itself to deep inner work and reflection, along with the purification of negative influences from your environment.

Utilize: This stone is particularly helpful for clearing your third eye chakra so that you can see things more clearly and through a compassionate lens. Start by doing a grounding meditation. Lie down, and pace the obsidian on your third eye chakra. Close your eyes, and envision its glassy black as water flowing over your third eye chakra; as you do, visualize a fog all around you lifting and your mind coming to clear focus.

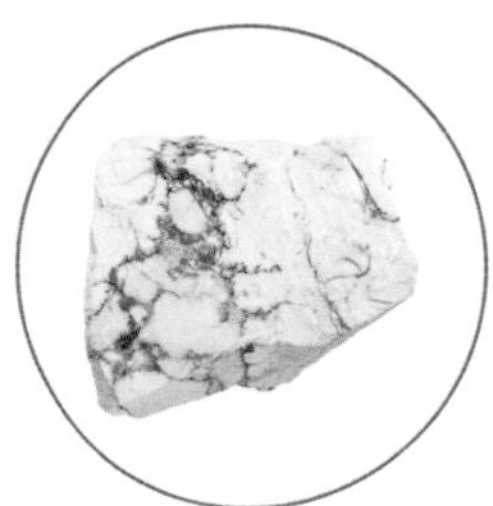

HOWLITE

Calming stone used to temper aggressive and disruptive emotions and ward off the same in your interactions. Creates an environment of patience, clearing communications of anxiety and tensions. Great for use during meditation, as it expands the consciousness and clears the mind. Also helpful in alleviating insomnia.

Utilize: This is a highly emotional stone but also protects us from spiritual blurred vision and promotes clarity and balance. Use your intuition to create a blessing for the stone that is specific to your needs. Once blessed, place the stone beneath your pillow for four full days during the waning moon cycle.

PYRITE

Stone of manifestation, luck, and abundance, and a psychic shield that protects the energy and environment of its bearer. Encourages the release of stagnant energy, allowing for unfettered creativity and the willpower to take bold actions in pursuit of goals and dreams.

Utilize: Begin by writing or journaling your current goal, whether that be protection, a new job, money, or anything your heart is telling you it needs. Hold a pyrite stone between your hands in a prayer position near your heart. Meditate on your goal by visualizing what it your life would look like once that goal has been achieved. Go into great detail, even visualizing what a whole new day with that goal accomplished would look like.

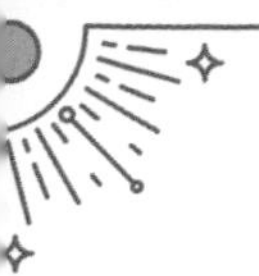

HEMATITE

Clears away stress and toxic impulses by drawing negativity from the auric fields. Naturally magnetic, it is said to bring equilibrium to the physical and spiritual realms. Used in shadow work, gently pulling past trauma to the surface, encouraging an honest look at subconscious patterns.

Utilize: The best way to harness the energy of this stone is through direct contact with your skin. Wear cleansed hematite as a bracelet so that you can always glance at it when you need an added boost.

FLUORITE

Strong shield from manipulation, and chakra and auric cleanser. Stabilizes emotions, clears feelings of guilt, anxiety, and tension. Establishes a strong connection to the intuitive mind, and creates a relaxed state for reasonable actions.

Utilize: This stone is very effective at assisting your third eye and calming emotional storms. Lie flat on your back, and place one stone on your heart and one on your third eye to assist in opening. Whisper or say aloud the following incantation: *I call on you, fluorite of truth, to open my vision wide.*

ATTRACTING LOVE SPELL

We all need a little love in our lives, whether you're seeking a new romance or reigniting long-lasting love. Turn to this spell when you feel that your attempts at finding or maintaining love have been unsuccessful and you need to raise the stakes.

Begin by gathering:

- **Blue lace agate for honest communication and building trust**
- **Amethyst to soothe conflict**
- **Garnet to stimulate passion and as a power boost**
- **Carnelian to open your heart and stimulate attraction**
- **Rose quartz to attract love**

STEP 1

Cleanse your crystals and place them in a sachet. Thank your crystals for their help, then recite the following spell, either whispered or spoken into the bag:

With honesty and grace, I attract my lover's embrace.

With passion that burns, to me you return.

Love now burns eterne.

STEP 2

Place the sachet under your pillow for one week.

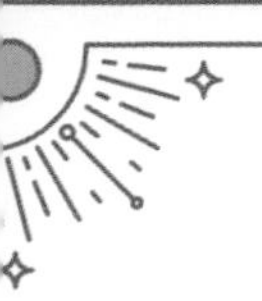

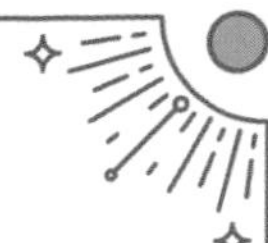

DIVINE PROTECTION SPELL

We all need protection, whether we're warding off illness, guarding ourselves and our homes against negative energy, or even blocking a curse. Use the following spell when things feel precarious but your efforts to resolve them have fallen short.

Begin by gathering:

* A white tea light candle for protection and purity
* Amethyst for energy protection
* Red jasper for courage and protection
* Clear quartz to ward off negativity and bring in light
* Black tourmaline for powerful protection
* Orange calcite to uphold and protect your mind, body, and spirit

STEP 1

Start by arranging your altar with the candle and light it. Hold each crystal, one by one, to the flame, close enough to slightly warm it, but not close enough to burn you. You can also use tongs here if it feels safer. As you hold up each one, recite the following spell:

Negativity is in the past,
dark feelings dissipate at last.
I call on the energy of these stones
to protect me and my home.

STEP 2

Let the candle burn out naturally.

VIBE CHECK

You'll need to listen to your intuition here so before answering these questions, do a breathing exercise and center yourself. Clear your mind and listen, then record your answers.

Where in your personal and professional environments do you feel the most stress and anxiety? What crystals are you called to use?

Is there anywhere that you feel would benefit from an energetic reset? What crystals are you called to use?

What will you do to incorporate the power of crystals in your daily life?

SPARK CREATIVITY

Where in your physical body do you feel stress the most? When you envision negative emotions, where do they live? Note on the below figure the areas you perceive these energies exist. You can use your art tools to color in different areas of the person below. Maybe a darker blue indicates negativity, or maybe bright yellow represents places of clarity and joy. You do you, and don't hold back.

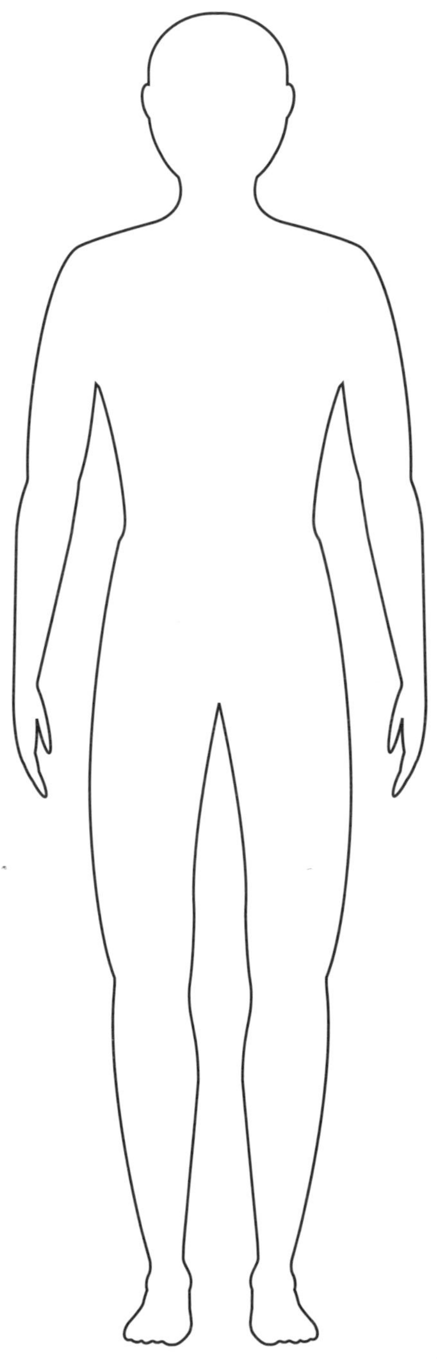

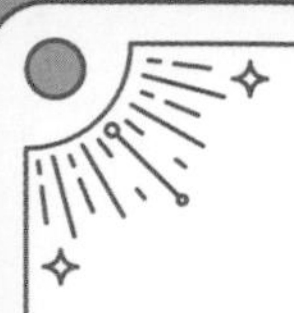

CRYSTAL GRIDS

Crystal grids help harness the powers that your crystals possess to aid in manifesting your desired intentions and spiritual goals. While there is no singular configuration for setting up a grid, designs are based around sacred geometric patterns. You can invest in a gridding board or find plenty of patterns with some research. You also have the option of freestyling your layout, creating your own pattern to support your intentions using your intuition. Additionally, you'll be provided with a few design options later in this section.

You'll need a variety of stones, with one acting as your central generator. This can be either a large crystal in a classic generator shape, which is a six-sided crystal with a central single termination point, or any crystal known for its high vibration. Clear quartz makes a powerful stand-in for the properties of all other stones. A variety of smaller crystals is then arranged to transmit your intentions and support the generator, creating a geometric pattern. Amplification stones can be used in creating an outer grid or as connecting points within the created pattern of your surrounding crystals. You may also incorporate personal items that possess particular emotional and energetic importance, or other materials, like flowers, shells, or candles. Let the pieces you're working with guide your design, and choose materials whose properties support your intentions. The selection of your layout and stones shouldn't be a point of stress; there is no such thing as perfection. Take your time, and enjoy the process. If you like, you can repeat a mantra, an affirmation, or a spell that is tailored to your personal needs and desires while you build your grid. Don't hesitate to call on your ancestors for guidance during this process in order to extract the most power from your grid.

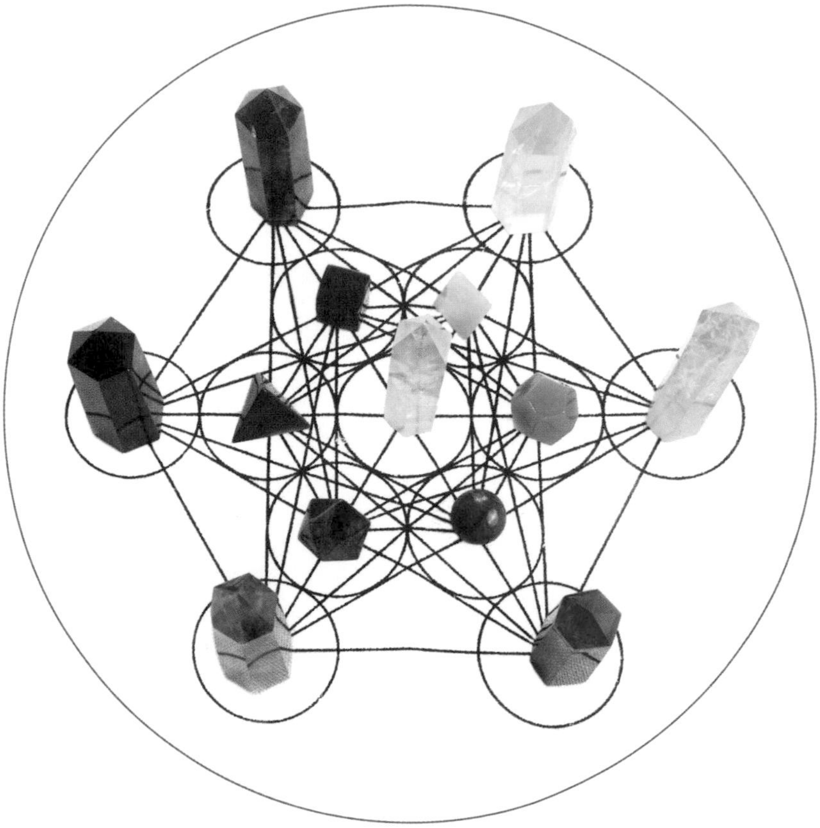

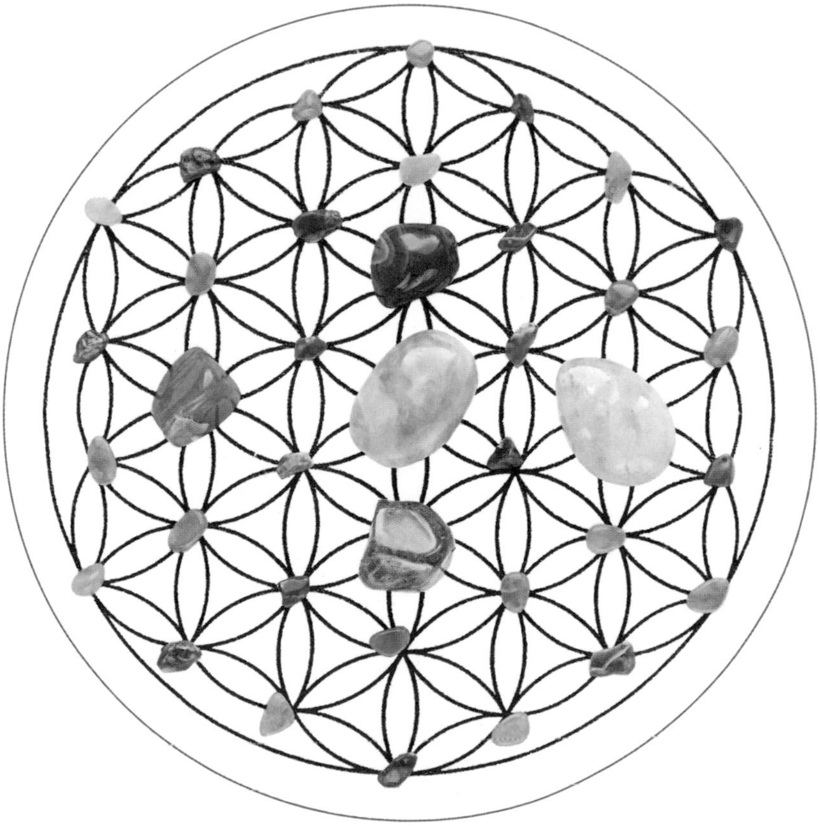

BUILDING CRYSTAL GRIDS

When building a crystal grid, it is important that you follow an established set of guidelines to properly harness and release its power.

STEP 1

Begin by establishing a space with a flat surface where your grid won't be disturbed. If you are able to create this near a window so that the sun and moon can shine on it and charge the crystals, even better! Cleanse the space, your crystals, and yourself, then record the date and tool you used in your cleansing log.

STEP 2

Do a mediation or breathing exercise while you focus on what purpose you want the grid to serve.

STEP 3

Program your crystals by holding them, either in groups or individually, in your hands while you visualize your goal, then speak your intention into the stones. If you wish, you can write your intention down and place the paper underneath your central crystal.

STEP 4

Select a central crystal that holds energies that are specific to your goal: citrine for manifestation, clear quartz for cleansing and banishing negative energy, rose quartz for love, and so forth. As you build, lay your crystals starting from the inside out, or outside in. This shouldn't be a random process. Do your best to keep the grid symmetrical. You can either lay your crystals on specific points according to your intuition, or at each point where the lines intersect and all outward points.

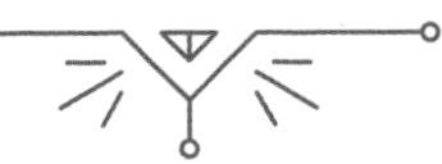

STEP 5

Activate your grid by tracing the shape of the pattern in the air with either a wand or your finger.

Leave the grid in place for anywhere between 48 hours and 40 days. During this time, if you feel that your grid might need a boost, you can retrace the pattern with your wand or finger, or write out your intention again with different wording every few days. You can also sit in front of the grid while you meditate so that the crystals can charge with your energies.

STEP 6

After this time ends, cleanse the crystals and space.

When in need of inspiration for creating your own crystal grids, turn to these established grid patterns. These grids are powerful conduits of crystal magic so it's important to know the specific purposes they hold.

VESICA PISCIS FOR MANIFESTATION

The Vesica Piscis symbol was first formed in nature as the basis of more complex pattern systems. This grid connects you with earth and goddess energies and is excellent for manifestation. It is also often used to invite feminine energies.

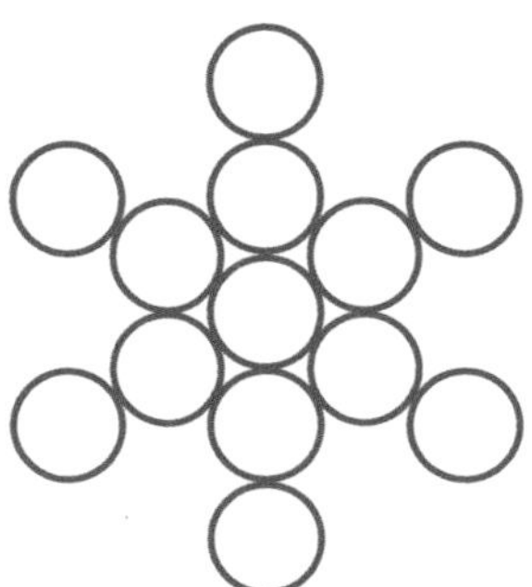

FRUIT OF LIFE ARRANGEMENT

The Fruit of Life crystal grid, also known as the Seed of Life, is used as a doorway to the divine. This symbol represents unlimited possibilities, new beginnings and new life paths. This is a powerful form for protection, balance, and while seeking the truth.

SEAL OF SOLOMON STAR

The Seal of Solomon Star is a healing grid, so this works well when built directly on the body. But if you have an unusual amount of ongoing stress and anxiety this also works well on your altar or a flat, cleansed surface.

FLOWER OF LIFE MANDALA

The Flower of Life Mandala represents the journey or cycle of one's life. This pattern built from several vesica pisces over-lapped and laid on top of each other is considered to be the very essence of Sacred Geometry in nature and the universe. Turn to this pattern when you're uncertain about specific areas of your life.

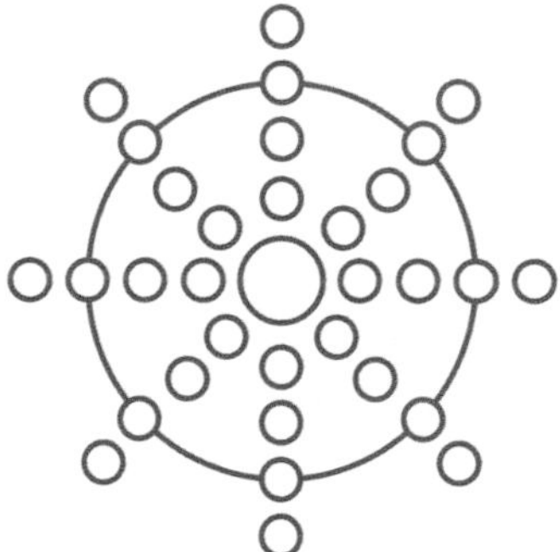

SUNBURST ENERGY CATCHER

A Sunburst Energy Catcher grid is meant to be used when you are in need of abundance, whether that be an abundance of money and good luck, love, joy; anything you might need a surplus of in your life. This can also be used to celebrate all the abundance already in your life.

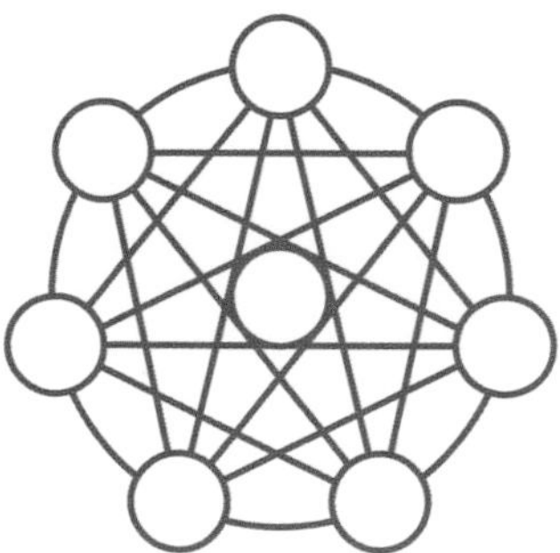

CHAKRA FOCUS PATTERN

The Chakra grid can be used to balance or cleanse your chakras. Use crystals whose colors represent the colors of each of the chakras. You can use a clear quartz as your central stone since it works to absorb negative energies and purify.

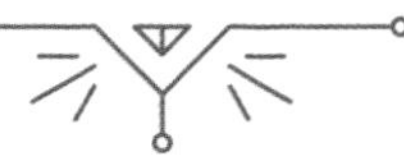

FREESTYLE DESIGN

Using your intuition, sketch your own crystal grid pattern.

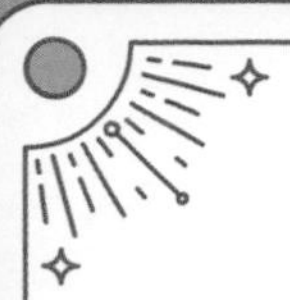

CREATE YOUR CRYSTAL GRID

STEP 1

Choose a design for your grid and the space in which you'd like to lay it out—somewhere that it will be undisturbed and has sufficient room to fit your design. Different grid shapes carry specific meanings. Squares establish boundaries and stability; circles are protective and unifying, symbolizing fertility and harmony; spirals are energetically expansive, associated with nature's golden ratio and universal spiritual connectivity; triangles represent structure and simplicity. More complex grids, like traditional sacred geometry patterns, build off of these rudimentary forms. Keep these grids in mind while you decide where to start, or refer here while developing patterns when you begin your grid.

STEP 2

Set your intention, focusing on what you feel is most needed in your life at the current moment. This may be manifesting luck and abundance, generating creative energy and inspiration, attracting love, or creating positive outcomes in situations you are working through. Be specific and optimistic about the energy you expect to receive. You can write the intention on a piece of paper and place it beneath your central crystal, or you could choose to speak this into the world with a personalized mantra, affirmation, or spell.

STEP 3

Choose your crystals. Consider how they support your intention and interact with one another. Select your central generator, ideally one that is larger than the surrounding crystals you plan on using. The rest is up to you in respect to color, shape, and quantity.

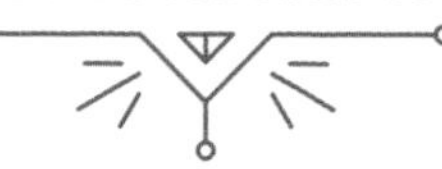

STEP 4

Cleanse your space and all crystals and materials you plan on utilizing. Use whatever method you prefer, including smudging with smoke, a spray, a solar or lunar bath, or your personal cleansing method.

STEP 5

Lay out the crystals. Use your intuition and allow for the flow of inspiration. You may decide to start from your central point and work your way out, build from the outer edges while making your way inward, or use a template design that you've acquired during your research. What is most important is keeping your intention in mind as you lay out your grid, not the order in which you do so.

STEP 6

Activate your grid, focusing again on your intention. You can do this with your hands, laying them over your grid to direct your energy into the design while repeating your mantra or spell. Other spiritual tools may be implemented in this step; pendulums and crystal wands are great choices for extending your intention to the completed grid. Visualize the connections being established and flowing from crystal to crystal. Take a moment to express gratitude to your design for the assistance it will provide in manifesting your goals.

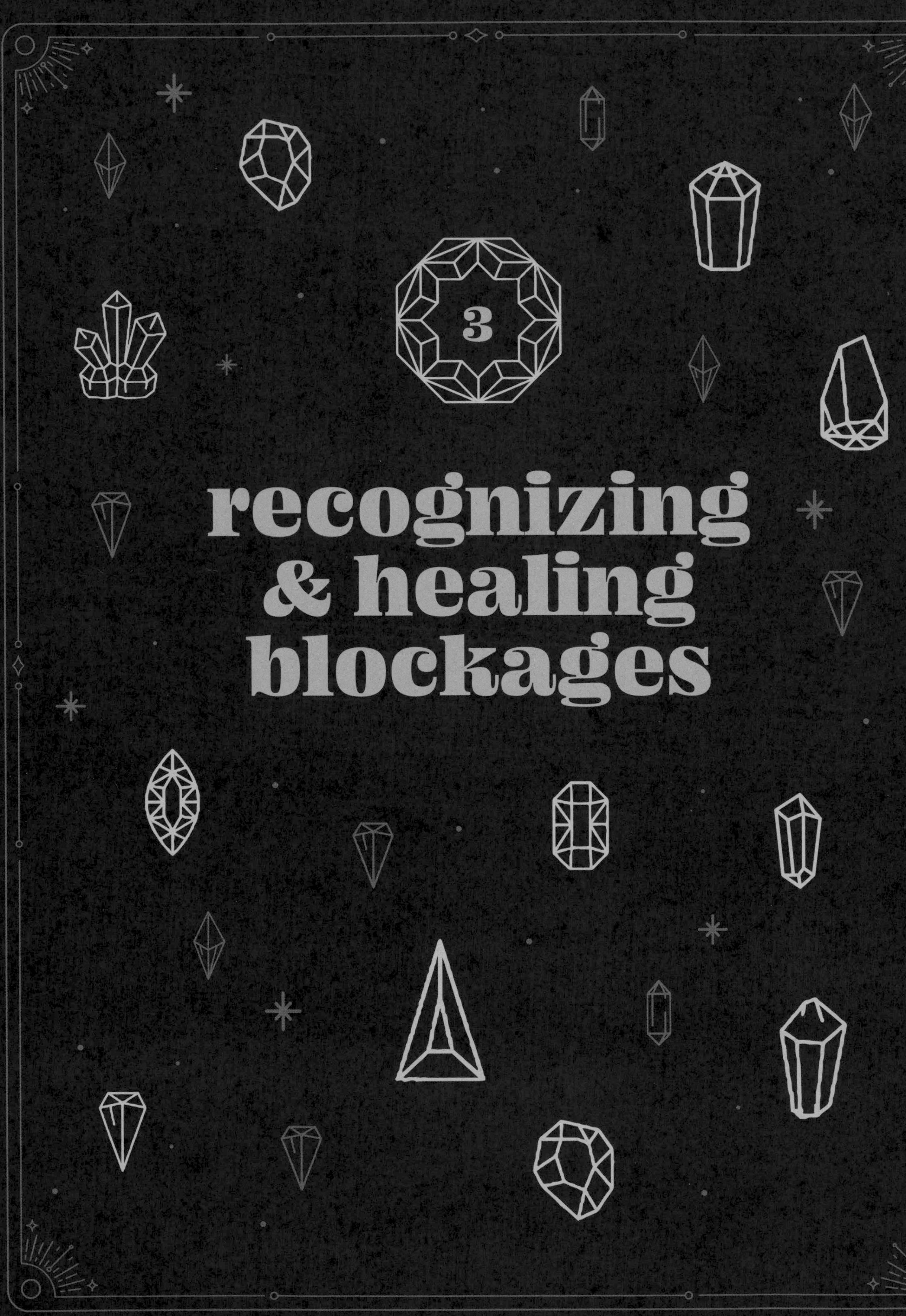

3

recognizing & healing blockages

There are times when we encounter resistance in our personal paths. These may be unhealthy patterns that we can't seem to escape in relationships, obstructed flow in creative endeavors, or even self-sabotage and impostor syndrome influencing professional progress. Negative mindsets and interrupted energetic flow can wreak havoc on the subconscious level, along with the spiritual and physical realms.

Negative energy and the disruption of the flow of chi (life energy) can manifest in anxiety, stress, disordered sleep, and a variety of physical and emotional discomforts. It can appear as low self-esteem, indecisiveness, or anger management issues. Recognizing blockages and working with intent to process and reflect on the shadow self can be a profound part of your spiritual journey. That might include confronting past trauma and recognizing our own roles in creating imbalanced energy within your life. Introspective analysis and meditation can be helpful in discovering the root and presence of energetic obstructions, paving the way to clearing psychic and spiritual pollutants.

One such way is to work with crystals to amplify and cleanse the seven main chakras each of us possesses. From crown to root, each correlates with an emotion, a color, an energy, and a ruling part of the body. Just as these different fields are associated with specific powers, so are crystals in terms of their ability to open and activate specific chakras. You'll know when it's time to sweep away those cobwebs as you see and feel the blockages physically and emotionally.

Please consult with professionals if you are experiencing serious emotional or physical problems. Crystals work in tandem with the physical world, so take pride in reaching out for help and use your crystals to support your care routine.

CHAKRA CORRELATIONS

Within each of us exist seven primary chakras, running from the base of our spines to the tops of our heads. Chakra means "wheel" in Sanskrit, as it was written in its first appearance in the ancient Indian Vedas sometime around 1500 and 500 BC. Prophets with the ability to see these energy fields say they appear as spinning funnels. They exist along the body in areas of concentrated energy, building in frequency upward from the earth to the heavens. In that same sense, they build from the corporeal to the ethereal foundations of the self.

THE SEVEN CHAKRAS

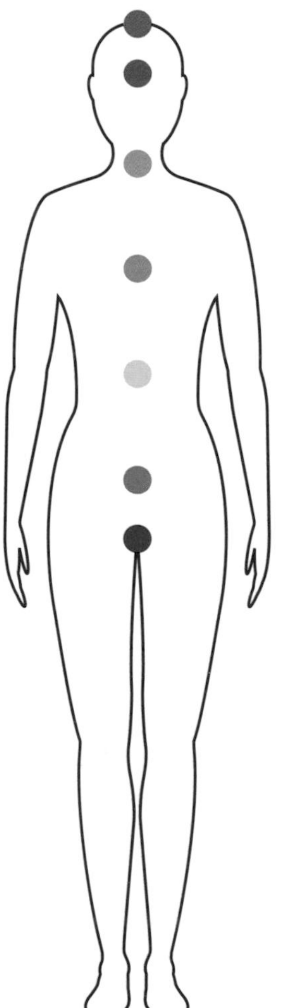

CHAKRA: Root
COLOR: Red
LOCATION: Base of the spine.
PROPERTIES: Rules stability, comfort and safety. Imbalance manifests as feelings of insecurity and anxiety about your needs being met.

CHAKRA: Sacral
COLOR: Orange
LOCATION: At the lower abdomen and spleen, just below the navel.
PROPERTIES: This rules over pleasure, creativity, and sexuality, thus influencing relationships. Out of balance, it will manifest as addictive behaviors, depression, sexual dysfunction, and creative blockages.

CHAKRA: Solar Plexus
COLOR: Yellow
LOCATION: At the diaphragm.
PROPERTIES: Rules over self-esteem, personal power, and personal responsibility. Imbalance manifests in feelings of fear, manipulative tendencies, and abuse of power.

CHAKRA: Heart
COLOR: Green
LOCATION: At the center of the chest.
PROPERTIES: Rules love, self-worth, compassion, and complex emotions. Imbalance brings depression, difficulty in relationships, and a lack of forgiveness. It is the astral plane, or bridge.

CHAKRA: Throat
COLOR: Blue
LOCATION: At the center of the throat and neck.
PROPERTIES: Rules over communication, independence, and the expression of personal and spiritual truths. Imbalance manifests as shyness, anxiety, arrogance, and misunderstandings.

CHAKRA: Third Eye
COLOR: Indigo
LOCATION: Between your eyebrows at the center of your forehead.
PROPERTIES: Rules over decision-making, intuition, and clarity of perception of self and others. Imbalance manifests as clouded judgment, lack of imagination, denial, pessimism, and a lack of purpose.

CHAKRA: Crown
COLOR: White and Lavender
LOCATION: At the top of the head.
PROPERTIES: The gateway to higher consciousness and divinity, and is connected to our circadian rhythms. Imbalance manifests as cynicism, disconnection from spirit as well as those around us, and dysfunctional sleep.

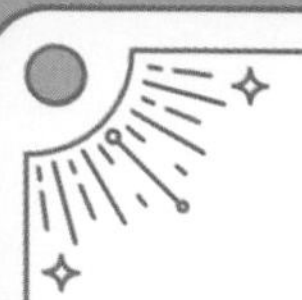

USING A PENDULUM

One way to locate a chakra imbalance is through the assistance of a crystal pendulum, known as dowsing. Your pendulum apparatus doesn't need to be a specific type of crystal but choosing crystals that clear negative energy are most effective. There are also pendulums made with multiple layered stones to mimic the colors of the chakras, which you can find online or at most mystic shops. Below are two methods you can use to work with the pendulum; one you can do with the help of a friend, and another that can be done solo.

When working solo, use a physical chart as a proxy by creating or printing a chakra chart that looks something like this:

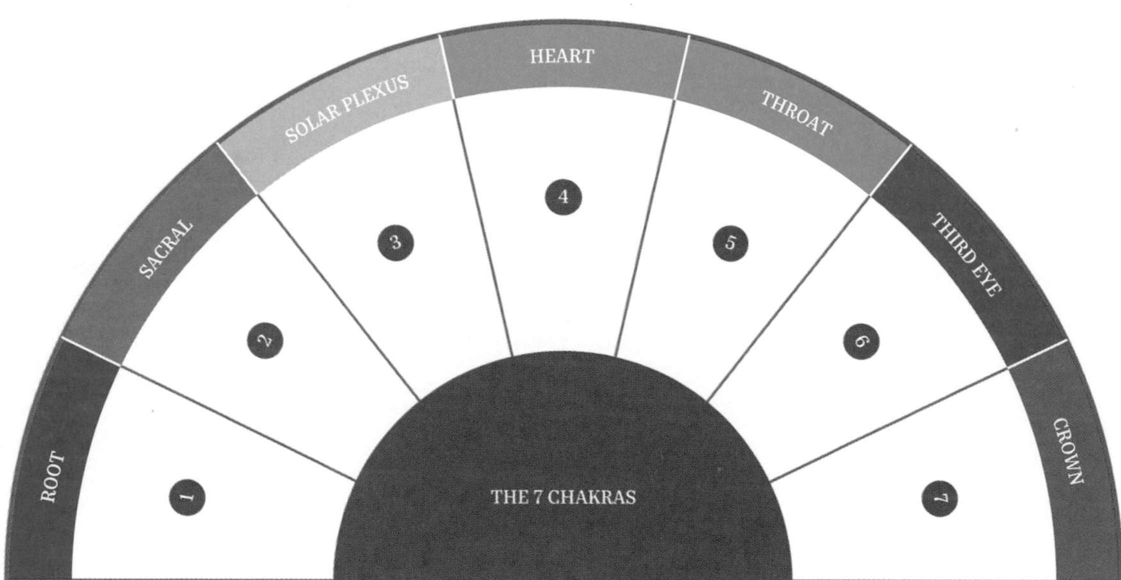

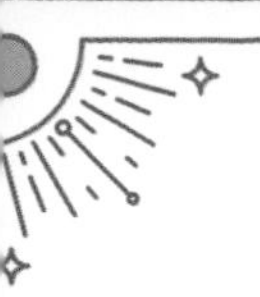

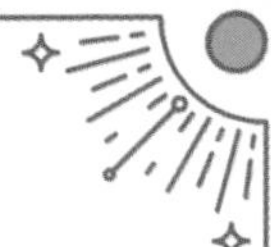

LEARN TO DOWSE

Dowsing is the action of dangling a pendulum over a chart, your hand, or in a space and asking a question, typically one that requires a yes or no answer. To figure out what motion indicates and 'yes' and which motion indicates a 'no,' dangle your pendulum over your palm and ask, "Show me yes." The pendulum will swing in a specific way: Maybe more to the right or more to the left, or in a circle. Then, do the same for 'no.' Note which movements indicate which answers, then begin your dowsing session.

SOLO

1. Use a proxy. This can be a chakra chart or the symbols of each chakra point.
2. Clear your mind. Enter this session with a fresh slate, eliminating your own bias from the outcome of your session.
3. Hold the pendulum over each section on the chart, taking a moment with each chakra. Then, dangle your pendulum over each section and ask, "Is this chakra blocked?"
4. Observe the direction and speed of your pendulum's movement and note whether you've received a yes or no answer..

WITH A FRIEND

1. Take a moment for a breathing exercise to clear your minds and center yourselves. You want to start without any bias so as not to influence the results of your session. Close your eyes and take a few deep breaths to release the energy of the day.
2. Once you feel relaxed, lie down on your back with your palms facing up, and close your eyes.
3. Have your friend hold the pendulum a few inches above your body, working its way up from root to crown and stopping at each chakra point.
4. Have your friend dowse over each chakra point and ask, "Is this chakra blocked?" Note your yes or no answers for each.
5. Turn over and check each chakra point from the back, again from root to crown. Note the movements of the pendulum and record your yes or no answers.
6. If you would like to get a more intricate reading, use the chart on p.86 to interpret specific messages from your pendulum.

INTERPRETING PENDULUM MOVEMENTS

Use the below chart to interpret your pendulum's movements.

↻	**Clockwise**	Chakra is open, energy flow is balanced and unobstructed
↺	**Counter-Clockwise**	Chakra is closed, energy is imbalanced or blocked
⟷	**Straight lines**	Partial blockage or imbalance
⬯	**Ovals**	Imbalance in flow specific to one side or the other
•	**Still**	Full blockage, no energy movement
⤻	**Big movements**	Greater flow of energy
⤻	**Small movements**	Weak flow of energy

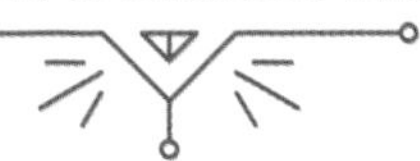

VIBE CHECK

Where in your body or spirit do you feel an imbalance? Where do you feel your strength?

Which specific chakras is your pendulum saying are currently blocked?

UNBLOCKING WITH CRYSTALS

Crystals serve as powerful assistants in the work of balancing and opening your chakras. They can be used to focus and strengthen the energy of individual chakras or aid in the alignment of your whole system. Chakras being organized by color is a fairly straightforward key to matching crystals to their areas of strength, though there are some variations and exceptions. On the next page, you'll find the primary chakras and some of their correlating stones, which can be used for opening and balancing their energy.

Make a list of the crystals you'd like to obtain when you're ready to clear your chakras.

1. **Chakra:** ....

   Crystals: ....

2. **Chakra:** ....

   Crystals: ....

3. **Chakra:** ....

   Crystals: ....

4. **Chakra:** ....

   Crystals: ....

5. **Chakra:** ....

   Crystals: ....

6. **Chakra:** ....

   Crystals: ....

7. **Chakra:** ....

   Crystals: ....

8. **Chakra:** ....

   Crystals: ....

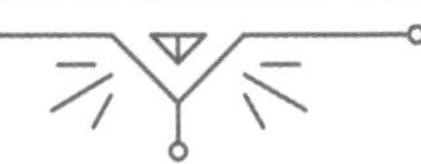

BLOCKED CHAKRA	COLOR
ROOT (MULADHARA)	**Red** Use red or black stones: Onyx, black tourmaline, red jasper, obsidian, garnet, bloodstone, bronzite, smoky quartz, ruby, and hematite
SACRAL (SWADHISTHANA)	**Orange** Use warm amber and orange stones: Carnelian, orange calcite, honey calcite, fire agate, citrine, sunstone, copper, and amber
SOLAR PLEXUS (MANIPURA)	**Yellow** Use yellow stones: Rutilated quartz, topaz, yellow aventurine, citrine, tiger's eye, septarian, fire opal, and pyrite
HEART (ANAHATA)	**Green** Use green or pink stones: Green aventurine, malachite, peridot, emerald, prehnite, green opal, amazonite, unakite, rhodochrosite, watermelon tourmaline, and rose quartz
THROAT (VISHUDDHA)	**Blue** Use blue stones: Sodalite, turquoise, lapis lazuli, apatite, chrysocolla, aquamarine, chalcedony, tanzanite, blue kyanite, dumortierite, celestite, and blue lace agate
THIRD EYE (AJNA)	**Indigo** Use indigo stones: Amethyst, lepidolite, purple fluorite, charoite, labradorite, moonstone, blue tiger's eye, apophyllite, angelite, and ammonite
CROWN (SAHASRARA)	**White and Lavender** Use white, purple, or multicolored stones: Clear quartz, herkimer diamond, rainbow moonstone, selenite, grape agate, howlite, white or black opal, pearl, angel aura quartz, sugilite, indigo gabbro, gold, diamond, and moldavite

BALANCING YOUR CHAKRAS WITH CRYSTALS

Choose a peaceful place where you won't be disturbed and do a meditation or breathing exercise to ground yourself.

STEP 1: Set up your chakra crystals, either arranged on a grid directly on your body or placed beside your body close to each corresponding chakra point.

STEP 2: Close your eyes and envision the root chakra flooded with a red light.

STEP 3: Let that light build and vibrate. Visualize how the corresponding crystal interacts with that energy. Feel the energy unblocking and clearing the space.

STEP 4: Stay with that chakra until it feels complete.

STEP 5: Work your way up through each chakra, visualizing the change of colors as the energy passes to the next.

STEP 6: When you reach the crown and complete your visualization, take a moment to feel the energy unified throughout your body. Imagine the light encompassing you. Take a deep breath and release it. Express gratitude for the moment.

STEP 7: Slowly begin to reawaken your awareness of your physical body, starting at your feet and working your way up to your crown chakra.

STEP 8: When you're ready, open your eyes. Take your time coming fully out of this moment.

STEP 9: Remove the crystals from near your body or from the grid, then cleanse them and the space.

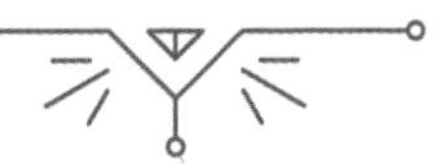

VIBE CHECK

Journal your experience, and go into as much detail as possible. What thoughts crossed your mind during your meditation? Where in your body did you feel the heaviest energy? Where does your body now feel most balanced? How do you feel physically? Are you lighter? Do you still feel blocked?

4

dreams & sleep

Many of us feel that we are trapped in a perpetual "hustle culture" cycle, where statements like "I'll sleep when I'm dead" are often touted as a badge of honor. But mental-health specialists, physicians, nutritionists, and fitness instructors across the board will tell you that sleep is just as essential to maintaining physical, emotional, and cognitive balance as what we eat or how many steps we take a day. The human machine needs rest in order to repair the damage of the day, consolidate memories, and process emotions. REM sleep, the final and deepest stage in the sleep cycle (which repeats multiple times throughout your sleep hours), provides stimulation to the parts of your brain that are most crucial to learning and memory. Insufficient sleep, insomnia, and disturbed cycles can leave you feeling cranky, sluggish, and mentally hazy.

So how do crystals play into all of this? They can aid in alleviating insomnia, stimulate dreams, and even assist in lucid dreaming. Are you aiming to calm your mind, or invigorate it with vibrant imagery? In this chapter, we'll explore your options for a more restful sleep and some techniques for getting more in touch with your dream world and the messages it conveys about your waking life.

SLEEP HYGIENE

Our sleep hygiene affects our waking lives profoundly. We need rest to perform at our emotional, intellectual, and physical best. But often, the chaos of our day—conflicts and stress of every variety—can prevent even the most well-intentioned bedtime plans from manifesting as an unobstructed sleep session. There are lots of ways that we can work towards our sleep goals and utilizing calming crystals is a great way to be mindful of these intentions. The following is a list of crystals to help alleviate insomnia and restless sleep. You may also look to stones that are closely associated with your higher chakras, as they will often also be of assistance in matters of the dream realm.

AMETHYST

Regarded as an "all-purpose" stone, amethyst helps relieve stress and still racing thoughts. Keep a stone by your bedside or under your pillow, or use it in your meditative practice before bedtime. With its strong connection to the third eye, it will bring clarity to your mind during your sleeping hours, potentially bringing a higher level of intuitive dreams.

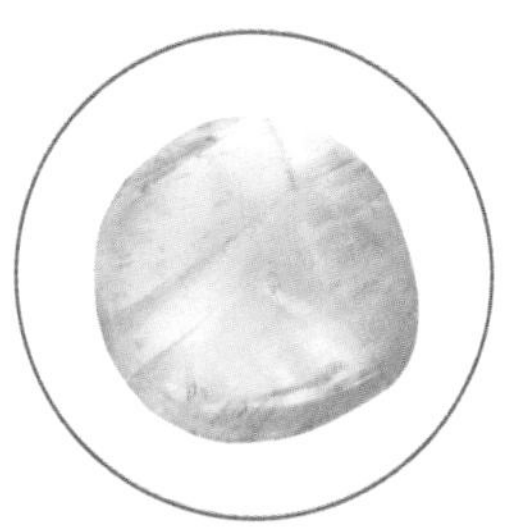

MOONSTONE

With its ability to alleviate stress, moonstone is another powerful sleep aid. As the name suggests, it is strongly associated with the powers of the moon and is said to shed light on our softer emotions. Place under your pillow or if small, balanced on your headboard above your head.

ANGELITE

Emitting the frequency of pure light, angelite is said to bring feelings of deep serenity and a connection to the spiritual realm. Astral-travel practitioners have been known to use this "stone of awareness" to assist in their journies. May also be used to experience vivid dreams. Place one stone at each of the four corners of your bed before sleep.

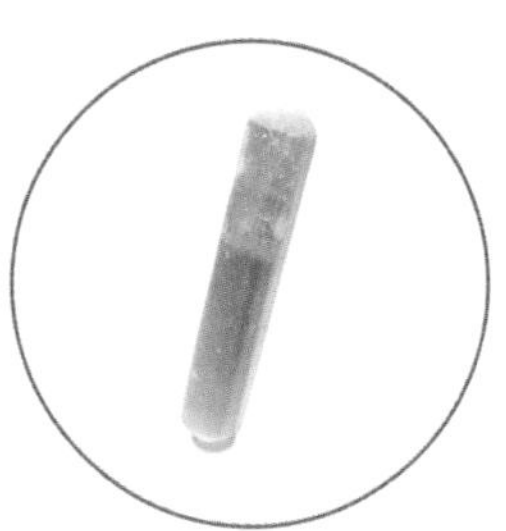

SELENITE

Known for its ability to cleanse negative energy from objects and spaces, selenite, sometimes called "liquid light," helps clear the mind of negativity and unblock stagnant energy that may be obstructing your sleep. Another high-frequency stone, it creates an atmosphere of tranquility and comfort. Selenite's clearing ability may also assist in minimizing snoring, which may serve as a second-hand sleep aid for whomever you share your space with. Place one stone under your pillow and one stone on the windowsills of your bedroom and home.

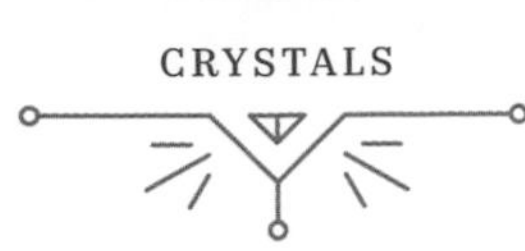

BLACK TOURMALINE

Another stone of powerful cleansing and protective ability, black tourmaline will eliminate negative energy within you as well as your environment. Said to stave off nightmares thanks to its reputation as a psychic shield, your mind will be at ease and secured against the effects of obstructive thoughts. Place stones in each corner of your bedroom, at the door, and under your pillow.

LEPIDOLITE

Encouraging feelings of love and compassion, lepidolite's ability to release tension and stress creates an ideal environment for restful sleep. The "peace stone," also known as the "stone of transition," will guide you into the dream realm with gentle ease and a boost of self-love. Place one stone beneath your pillow and one stone at the foot of the bed.

SMOKY QUARTZ

Great for calming the mind and body, smoky quartz will help dissolve emotional blockages and fend off negative energy that may be keeping you awake. A strong tool for grounding, it will bring stillness to your energy and is said to dispel nightmares. Place one stone in areas of your bedroom that are important to you. If you have a special chair, place one on it; if you have an altar, place one there. You can also place one on your bedside table or simply at the top of the bedroom doorframe.

HOWLITE

Often utilized to calm the mind during meditation practices, howlite will bring that same serene energy to your sleep. By slowing down frantic thoughts and emotions, your system will be encouraged to enter a restful space with ease. Place one howlite on each corner of your bed and one under your pillow.

ROSE QUARTZ

Strongly associated with matters of the heart, rose quartz fills the spirit with feelings of love and compassion. By strengthening our ability to experience positivity and forgiveness, it becomes easier to release disappointment and frustrations that may have gathered in the day. Make a cup of a restful tea such as chamomile or lavender. Cleanse your rose quartz, then place in the bottom of your teacup. Drink slowly before bed.

CELESTITE

A third eye stone, celestite is linked to the celestial, infusing our energy with grace and a desire for inner peace. Said to expand our intuitive ability, its connection to the astral realm makes for powerful dream recall. Place three celestite stones at the head of your bed, either under the pillow or on the bedframe. Then place one on each side of the bed and three at the foot.

When working with crystals to assist you in your pursuit of healthy sleep, remember that less is more. Mixing too many materials can overcrowd your energy and make you more restless. Always remember to cleanse your crystals after use to keep them in peak performance and free of negative residue.

VIBE CHECK

Now that you've worked with crystals to aid your sleep, record your observations. Which crystals felt like they lulled you with ease? Which seemed to influence your dreams? Are you waking up feeling recharged?

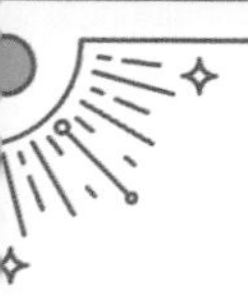

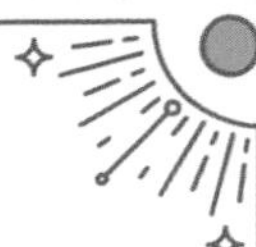

SPELL TO PROMOTE RESTFUL SLEEP

If you've been having an especially hard time sleeping lately, perform this spell to promote healing rest. Don't forget to start with a meditation or breathing practice to clear mental clutter and open yourself.

Begin by gathering:

* **4 pocket-sized mirrors**
* **2 stones each of moonstone, smokey quartz, lepidolite, clear quartz**

STEP 1

Cleanse your mirrors, stones, bed, and the whole room with your go-to cleansing method. If you're using incense, crack a window so that the negativity can escape as the smoke clears. Once the space is cleansed, close the window.

STEP 2

Place one mirror in each corner of the room facing outward so that the mirror will block any negative energies and anxieties from entering your cleansed space.

STEP 3

Place the moonstones in front of one mirror, the lepidolite stones in front of another mirror, and so forth with the remaining stones so that the mirror traps their energies in your room.

STEP 4

As you tuck in and fall asleep, repeat the chant, *I am at peace, I am at rest, I have beautiful dreams, and wake up refreshed.*

CRYSTALS FOR DREAMWORK

You've got your sleep hygiene in order and dreamtime has become plentiful. But now you'd like to delve deeper. What tools could you use to amplify those dreams and capture them better? Dreams are closely related to the astral plane, along with the subconscious mind, so stimulating your higher chakras is key. You can help influence your dream output, or even explore some lucid dreaming techniques, with intention, focus, and patience. Incorporating crystals can also bring focus to your dreams.

LODOLITE

Also known as the shamanic dreamstone, this variety of quartz includes a number of inclusions that can make it appear to have full worlds within it (It comes as no surprise then that it's also referred to as landscape, scenic, or garden quartz). Long utilized for divination and scrying, this material is used for past-life recall, hypnosis, and, of course, dreamwork. You should cleanse and program your lodolite before sleep so that it can help you recall and record your dreams. If you find yourself having trouble remembering, use the stone the next morning in meditation to help stimulate your memory.

HERKIMER DIAMOND

Used to assist with clairvoyance and clairaudience, herkimer diamonds are linked to the third eye chakra. They are deeply calming and help facilitate lucid dreaming and dream recollection. They assist easing the passage into higher states of consciousness.

LAPIS LAZULI

Popular as a strong conduit for psychic energy and intuitive abilities, this cubic crystal has been prized throughout time for its dazzling color. Said to help in accessing your Akashic records (universal knowledge of past, present, and future). Used to manifest lucid dreaming, as it promotes a deep mental clarity and the opening of the third eye.

MOLDAVITE

A rare and notoriously powerful tektite, moldavite is formed via meteorite impact and can be dated back 15 million years. Believed to be one of the world's oldest and most powerful minerals, moldavite should not be used by novices. It is great for dream journeying, and practitioners are strongly encouraged to use it simultaneously with a strong grounding stone like hematite or red jasper to help neutralize the intensity of its power. Moldavite shows you what you need and pulls no punches.

LABRADORITE

A highly spiritual stone, this iridescent mineral assists with dream recall and lucid dreaming, and works as a strong guide within your dreams. Will protect you from nightmares and prevent sleepwalking while also working on recharging and balancing your energy as you sleep. Stimulates a strong connection with the spiritual realm.

BLUE APATITE

Also called the stone of manifestation, this mineral influences dreams and helps you retain and retrieve details. Blue apatite is said to promote prophetic dreams and aid in astral travel and lucid dreaming. Supports the third eye along with the throat chakra, and it nurtures and uplifts the consciousness.

AZURITE

Praised for heightening intuitive ability, powers of imagination, and ease of astral travel, azurite is the "stone of heaven." This is a high-frequency stone linked strongly to the crown chakra that has historically been used to access spirit guides and as a key to the Akashic records. Works to help integrate knowledge from the spiritual realm into our present lives.

LUCID DREAM EXERCISE

Be mindful of the value and fragility of the crystals you choose to work with. While some are perfectly safe and secure under your pillow or on your bedside, like tumbles and palm stones, you should use your discretion. You can use these stones in preemptive meditation or find them in beaded specimens on bracelets that are safe to wear during sleep.

STEP 1

Lie down in bed and close your eyes. Do a meditation or breathing exercise.

STEP 2

Place your chosen crystal on your third eye point.

STEP 3

Visualize the energy of the crystal interacting with your own. Focus on your intentions for this session and the work you aim to accomplish.

STEP 4

When you feel ready, open your eyes and remove the crystal. Place it somewhere safe—on your headboard, under your pillow, or worn as a bracelet—and settle into sleep.

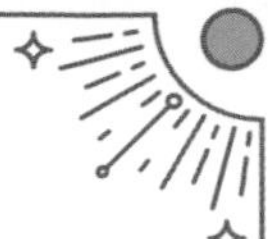

VIBE CHECK

What do you hope to encounter in your dreams, or what knowledge are you seeking?

Reflecting on your most recent dream memory, what do you believe the message was in the dream?

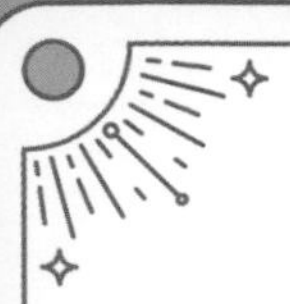

DREAM JOURNAL

While working with the various crystals mentioned in this section, it's a great idea to keep a dream journal to collect the imagery and emotions you encounter. You can keep a small notebook by your bed, or even capture some voice notes on your phone. But get in the habit of logging these details as soon as you wake up, since it is not uncommon for them to fade quickly. You can start your practice below to help establish your routine. Continue this journal in the back of the book or establish a dedicated dream journal.

Date: ....

Crystal used: ....

Dream and emotion experienced: ....

....

....

Date: ....

Crystal used: ....

Dream and emotion experienced: ....

....

....

Date: ....

Crystal used: ....

Dream and emotion experienced: ....

....

....

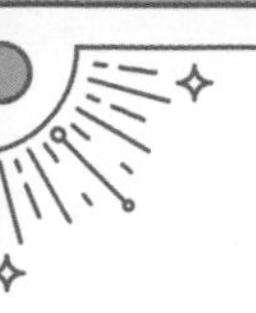

Date:

Crystal used:

Dream and emotion experienced:

Date:

Crystal used:

Dream and emotion experienced:

Date:

Crystal used:

Dream and emotion experienced:

Date:

Crystal used:

Dream and emotion experienced:

5

crystals for romance & self-love

Love is a bottomless well of mystery and reward within each of our lives. It is the most powerful force that exists, which is why we will focus on it in this chapter. We are always seeking love, working on maintaining it, learning how to give and receive it, and processing how to release it before starting the cycle anew. As we grow and change, we learn to love ourselves through each new phase of our lives. Love isn't just a feeling, it's an action—a decision we make to actively share warmth, affection, joy, and our inner workings—that we bestow on ourselves and others.

Let's explore some crystals that can assist in drawing in the energy of love and how we can exercise those actions. We'll discuss how to open our hearts to better receive love from others as well as ourselves, and amplify passion and compassion. Don't worry, we'll also get into detaching for those moments when love is no longer enough.

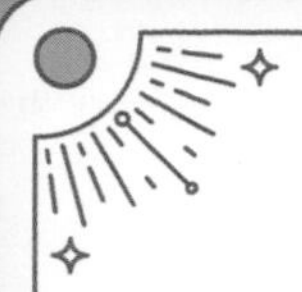

SPARKING PASSION

When you think of the physical act of love, what comes to mind? Is it intimate engagement with another or yourself? What senses are involved? There are many ways you can approach the invigoration of your desire. There are various meditations, and yogic practices you can explore to awaken your kundalini energy, regarded as the "coiled snake" of latent divine feminine energy, located at your root chakra on the base of your spine. It is said that when this "snake" uncoils, the energy flows freely upward through each of the seven main chakras, starting from your root and shooting upward to the heavens.

Our desire is our primal engine, driving us toward sensual fulfillment. It exists within us even if sometimes it may seem dormant, curled up somewhere deep where we can't see it. Refer to the following list for materials to turn to when you need to awaken your libido or reignite that spark.

SERPENTINE

Considered a key stone in awakening your kundalini energy safely. The "snake stone" works with all chakra points to unblock energy and insulate the aura. It boosts our ability to feel compassion and express loving emotions unencumbered.

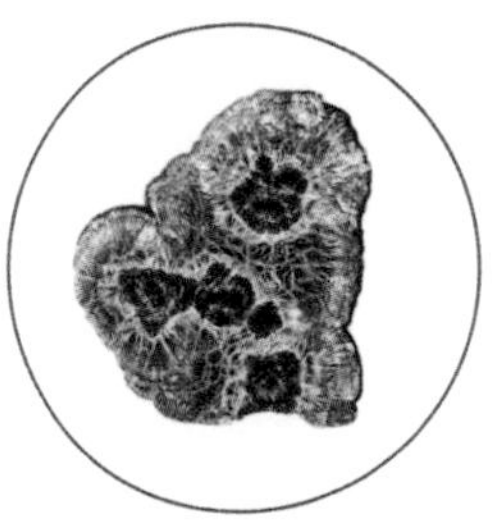

SERAPHINITE

Deriving its name from *seraphim*, or angel, it links your earthly form to the angelic realm, working on all chakras to heal and release energy that no longer serves you. Bringing you into harmony with the divine, your passions can feel regenerated, and its loving effect on you will be mirrored in those you encounter.

ETHIOPIAN OPAL

An emotional intensifier, commonly referred to as a Welo opal, it brings true nature to the surface, amplifying psychic abilities and igniting passion. Boosts creativity and releases inhibitions.

SHIVA LINGAM

Found only in the Namada, one of India's sacred rivers, this stone is said to represent the phallus (lingam) of Lord Shiva. Amplifier of fertility, sexuality, and balance for the physical and emotional self.

CUPRITE

Also known as red copper ore, this stone brings vitality and strengthens the root chakra, working as an overall grounding force. This is a powerful fertility stone, activating feminine energy and supporting overall reproductive and sexual health.

FIRE AGATE

A powerful aid to shake you out of a rut during periods of stagnation, the fiery nature of this stone energizes the sacral chakra, the ruler of sexuality and creativity. Said to heighten stamina, stimulate fertility, aid in correcting sexual dysfunction, and ease worries surrounding intimate relationships.

GARNET

Revered since ancient times as a regenerative stone. Said to revitalize and attract passion and love and activate kundalini energy. Intrinsically tied to the act of physical love, it is said to increase libido and dissolve emotional blockages, opening you up to feelings of self-confidence and connection to the present moment.

CARNELIAN

Another ancient talisman said to help with manifesting goals, especially those of fertility, this formidable stone helps reinforce love within relationships, invigorates energy of sacred sex, and works to heal trauma. Motivation, performance, and endurance are all supported by this stone.

If you feel like you need to be more proactive than simply placing crystals in your bedroom, try the following spells.

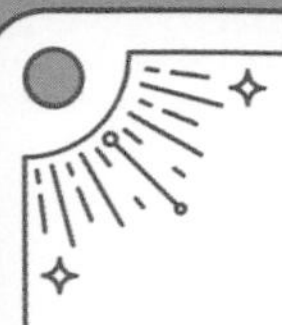

SPARK PASSION SUGAR SCRUB

This bathtime scrub is infused with the magical properties of crystals and essential oil, designed specifically to spark physical intimacy. The brown sugar is less toxic than bleached white sugar, and the tiny grains will exfoliate to make your skin baby soft.

Begin by gathering:

* **A cleansed jar with a lid for sealing**
* **Brown sugar, to gently exfoliate**
* **A skin-safe carrier oil (coconut oil or olive oil is a great option)**
* **Ylang ylang essential oil, a powerful aphrodisiac**
* **One each of the following crystals, small enough to fit in the jar: red tiger's eye, fire agate, carnelian, and rose quartz**

STEP 1

After cleansing all your materials, fill your jar halfway with the brown sugar.

STEP 2

Fill the rest of the jar with your skin-safe carrier oil, leaving about 2 inches of free space at the top.

STEP 3

Add as many drops of the ylang ylang as you wish. Start with 3 drops and work your way up from there until you have your desired scent strength.

STEP 4

Stir your ingredients together, then nestle your crystals in the scrub to infuse their energies with the concoction.

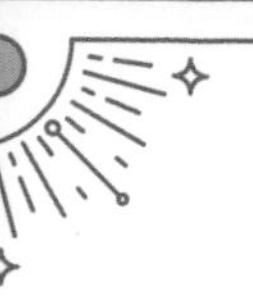

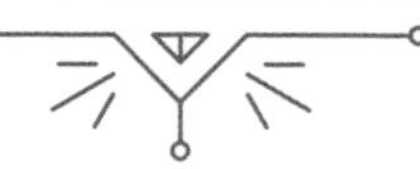

STEP 5

Use on your body while in the bath or shower. Be careful! It makes the ground very slick.

STEP 6

Place the lid on the jar between uses. Sugar acts as a preservative, so this has a long shelf life.

GET IN THE MOOD RITUAL

One of the most important components of sparking intimacy is to make sure you and your space are comfortable and calm. Don't forget your meditation or breathing exercise before you start.

Begin by gathering:

* **Your cleansing tools (incense or spray work well here, as they infuse the whole space)**
* **A sachet bag (satin works well since it is a sensual material)**
* **One of each, small enough to fit in the sachet: rose quartz, opal, garnet, cuprite**
* **A pinch each of dried basil, lavender, and rosemary to boost the energies of the crystals**
* **1 red candle to ignite passion**

STEP 1

Start by cleansing your bedroom. Be sure to crack a window to allow negative energy to flow out.

STEP 2

Make sure the bed is made, the sheets are clean, and the lights are turned low.

STEP 3

Place the crystals and herbs in your sachet.

STEP 4

Arrange the sachet next to the candle.
As you light the candle, recite:

As crystals grow and herbs do bloom,
infuse with passion this holy room.
Sensuality and ardor burn within,
as love and desire live herein.

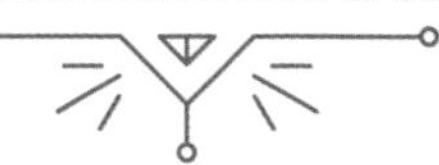

CREATE A PASSION GRID

Another way to ignite passion is to create an intentional crystal grid.

STEP 1: Prepare an altar for your crystal grid. If you already have an altar, clean, organize, and cleanse it before laying out your grid. If you don't have a dedicated altar, then you can create a temporary one by finding a space with a flat surface where it won't be disturbed. Clear all clutter from the surface then give it a spiritual bath with your cleansing tool.

STEP 2: Choose your crystals. Using this book and your intuition as a guide, pick a central crystal to represent your main intention. Then, choose crystals to support and bolster your central crystal.

STEP 3: Use the space below to plan and sketch out your Passion Grid. This is a good opportunity to use your paints, colored pencils, markers, or crayons to represent the crystals you'd like to use in your grid so you can get an idea of what it will look like aesthetically.

STEP 4: Perform a breathing exercise or a meditation to infuse your crystals and grid with your intention. Then, take this page to your altar and lay out your grid.

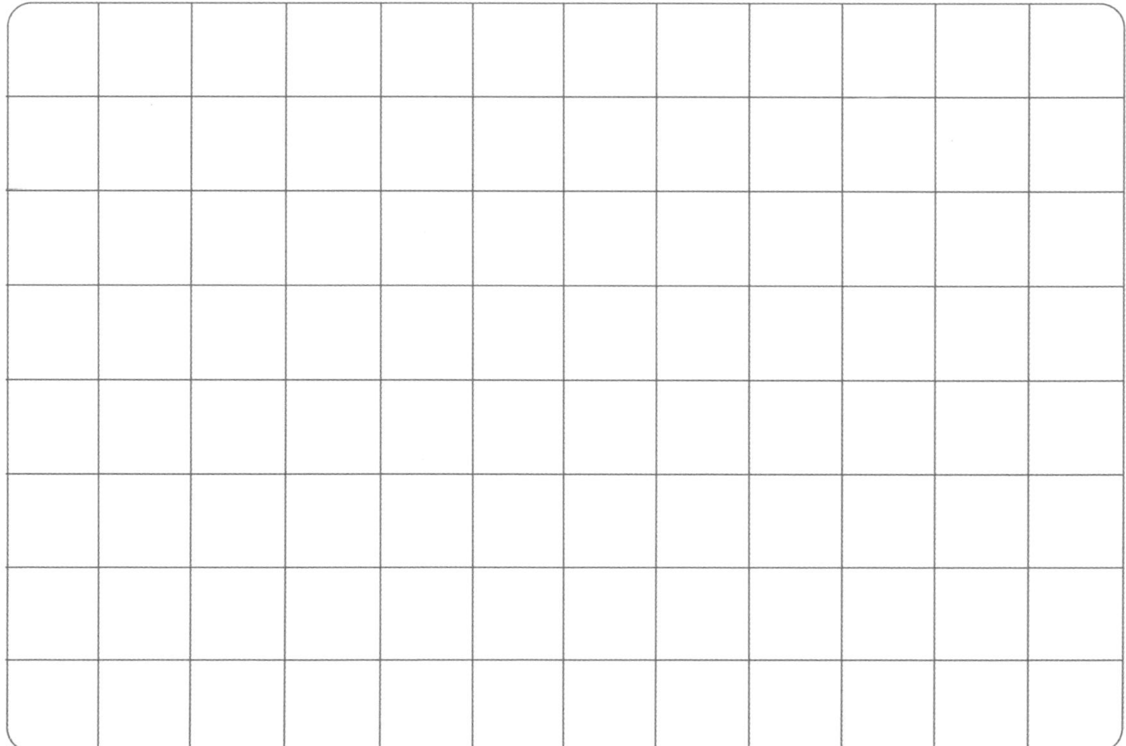

GIVING AND RECEIVING LOVE

As important as physicality is, love extends far beyond the sensual. Ideally, it is at the root of our friendships, familial exchanges, worldviews, and the tones of our inner voice. Sometimes, though, the stress of life catches up to us, and we close ourselves off. When we start becoming closed off or blocked, feelings of frustration arise, making our fuses short, tempers flaring, and our patience worn thin. Our relationships begin to crumble, and we are stunted in giving and receiving love. So how, in times like these, can we expand our heart space and reopen ourselves to joyful reciprocity? Turn to some of the following stones to help unblock and open yourself to giving and receiving love.

KUNZITE

Connecting the heart and the mind, this powerful stone of divine love opens you to freely reciprocate and receive loving energy. This crystal works to banish feelings of mistrust and shadows lingering in the auric space. Assisting in healing emotional wounds, kunzite nurtures your growth, encouraging feelings of self-worth and self-love.

ROSE QUARTZ

A stone of unconditional love, the energy of rose quartz promotes deep healing and strengthens vibrations of self-love. It encourages healing communication and attracts and strengthens emotional connections. Self-care can also be aided with this crystal, being popular with practitioners who seek to integrate its benefits into skin-care routines via facial rollers and gua sha or added to an elixir to promote a youthful complexion.

ALEXANDRITE

Promotes feelings of self-esteem and deeper appreciation for those in your life. It is a high-vibration stone that spreads feelings of joy, connects the root, heart, and crown chakras, and promotes intuitive harmony, healing, and luck. Those looking for deep soul connections are said to attract their mates with this stone.

PINK TOURMALINE

Emits strong energies of balance and healing. Said to fill you with the light of love, this crystal reinvigorates your passion for life and renews your sense of purpose. Also used to relieve deep emotional pain and ease feelings of anxiety and depression, this is a powerful tool for amplifying feelings of self-love and compassion.

RUBY FUCHSITE

Sometimes called the ultimate heart stone, this rare crystal combines ruby and fuchsite for a dual-action approach. The ruby brings to the table the powers of strength, zest for life, and courage, while fuchsite manifests inner peace, compassion, and nurturing energies. Joined together in a single stunning crystal, making this stone a formidable force that encourages self-love, cleanses emotional residue, and initiates heart-opening.

EMERALD

The stone of successful love, emeralds draw energies of loyalty and universal love. Encourages the full appreciation of life and its pleasures and works to heal emotional and spiritual pain. This opening stone preserves existing relationships, inspires truthful communication, and enhances intuition.

VIBE CHECK

Think about your current emotional state and the state of your relationships then answer the following questions.

Has your patience been running thin? Are you short and snappy with loved ones and the people you encounter? Have you been quick to anger or defensive? If you answered yes, write about the last time you felt like your true self and at peace.

What negative emotions are you now experiencing? How have they affected your relationships?

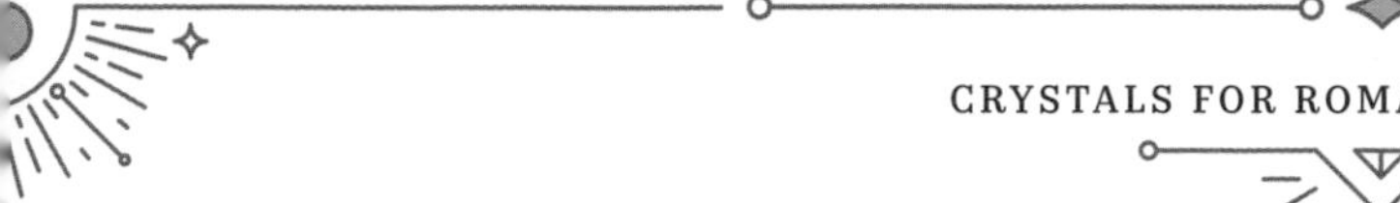
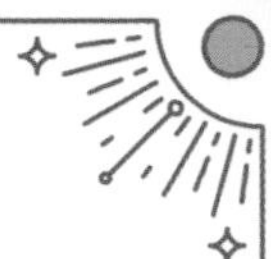

CLEAR BLOCKAGES RITUAL

Reflecting on your answers, look over the list of opening crystals (pages 14-15), and choose one that speaks to you and your current state. Use the following ritual to clear blockages and manifest love.

STEP 1

Sitting or lying down in a comfortable position (after a meditation or breathing exercise), hold your chosen crystal against your heart chakra, warming it with your hands and fusing your energy with its own.

STEP 2

Close your eyes and take a few deep, cleansing breaths.

STEP 3

Reflect on your needs. Visualize the specifics of what you need and want to manifest.

STEP 4

Hold the crystal to your mouth and speak your needs into it, programming your intention into the stone.

STEP 5

Open your eyes and place the crystal beside you.

STEP 6

Write down your desires and intentions on a piece of paper. Be detailed about what you want and don't want.

STEP 7

Fold the paper and place it under your crystal.

STEP 8

Speak words of gratitude to your crystal and your guide for assisting you in your pursuits.

STEP 9

Leave the intention uninterrupted under the crystal. Revisit it during the next moon cycle.

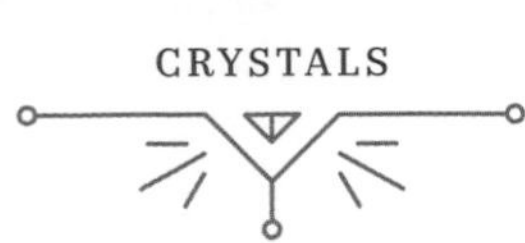

INTEGRATING CRYSTALS INTO YOUR SELF-CARE

Loving yourself is much more difficult than it sounds. We are our own worst critics and tend to be hard on ourselves. But loving yourself is necessary in order to give and receive love with others. Although challenging, it's vitally important that we spiritually care for ourselves by allowing self-forgiveness, believing in ourselves, trusting our intuition, and of course, practicing self-care.

Self-care can mean different things to different people, but there are many ways to let yourself know that you deserve love.

- **Establish a nightly routine in which you carve out time to celebrate your wins for the day.**
- **Develop a solid morning routine, making sure to start with gratitude and acknowledgment of things you're thankful for.**
- **Do something nice for yourself at least once a day, keeping the focus on being kind.**
- **Get intricate by integrating water-safe non-porous crystals into your bathing rituals (see Spark Passion Sugar Scrub, page 110) or by using gua sha or facial rollers.**
- **Prioritize time for an aromatherapy or herbal bath infused with the power of crystals specifically chosen to balance your energy.**
- **Energy loves movement, so schedule time in each day, even just five minutes, to move around so that energy can pass through you. I love a good yoga session with my chosen crystals lining the top of my mat. Self-care takes work, but it is a labor of love.**

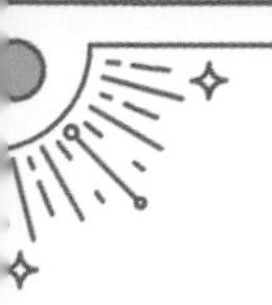

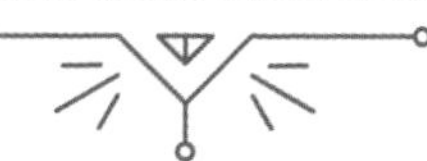

Here are some suggestions on incorporating the power and energy of crystals into your self-care routine:

GUA SHA

Originating in China, the word gua sha is derived from the Chinese word for "scraping." The tools come in a range of stone options, most commonly rose quartz and jade, so choose one that best emits the energies that you require. After cleansing your face, apply a facial oil before using the tool to gently scrape your skin. For an added boost, infuse the oil with a skin-safe essential oil like lavender.

FACIAL ROLLER

Similar to gua sha, but with a rolling rather than a scraping action, facial rollers are growing in popularity as a self-care tool. They can most commonly be found carved from rose quartz, jade, clear quartz, or obsidian. For a refreshing, skin-firming boost, keep it in the refrigerator between uses.

CRYSTAL-INFUSED BATH

Water is a powerful purifier, and nothing relaxes like a nice, warm bath. Add water-safe crystals directly in the bathwater, or arrange them around the edges of the tub so that you can bask in their energy as you soak. You can also add calming herbs or essential oils to the water, which carry their own magical properties and work in tandem with the energies of the crystals. If you're in need of a little fun, add a bath bomb or bubbles!

SLEEP

Giving yourself enough rest and encouraging good sleep are essential to being your authentic self and loving who you are. Since your subconscious is incredibly active as you sleep, choose a crystal that has the properties that you need replenished, and place it beneath your pillow or near your bed. For more on crystals and healthy sleep, refer to Chapter 4 (page 92).

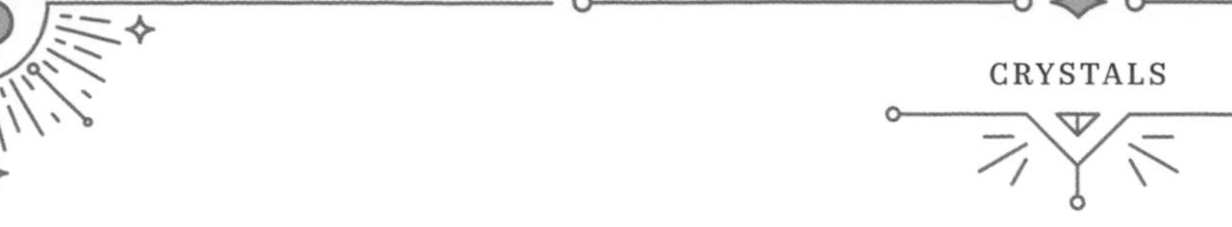

WORRY STONES

Sometimes, one worrisome thought leads to another, and then another, and before you know it, you're tumbling down a rabbit hole of anxiety. When you catch yourself doing this, it's often helpful to carry a crystal with you wherever you go so that you can palm or rub the stone to release its energy and remind you to stay calm. Choose a crystal whose properties are soothing to you. Then, choose a smooth shape. This can be in a heart, in an indented oval, or maybe a sphere; use your intuition. No matter what shape you choose, it's important that it is perfectly smooth on the surface, as this tactile experience will help create feelings of peace.

Another use is to incorporate it into your meditation practice. When you first learned to meditate on page 25, the focus was on the shape of the crystal. A worry stone meditation uses a similar process. Citrine, opal, and amethyst are all great choices for their grounding properties, as well as their promotion of self confidence and love. Choose an affirmation that speaks to your current situation and repeat this "mantra of the moment" each time you run your fingers over the worry stone.

GET A MOVE ON

Your body is full of energy that wants to move: move throughout, move out of, and move into you. When we start snapping at our loved ones, begin creating conflict, and have an overall restless feeling, it means it's time to move that energy around. We don't all have time or finances to join a gym or take regular exercise classes, and many of us simply don't connect with a regimented routine. Motivate yourself to move by making it free and fun and get that energy flowing!

- **Take the dog for extra-long walks. Dogs bring so much joy to our lives and if you can laugh a bit or delight in their antics while burning some energy that's ideal! If you don't have a dog but you enjoy their company and want the excuse to move a bit, volunteer to walk a friend's dog. Or even take on a side-job as a neighborhood dog walker and earn a little extra money while you're at it.**
- **Go jump in a lake. Or a river, or a pool. Swimming is a highly aerobic exercise that moves energy very effectively. It requires movement of every muscle in your body and it increases the oxygen in your system, increasing feelings of serenity.**
- **Do free yoga or qi gong sessions online. There are countless video platforms that offer free classes in the comfort of your own home. These are great when you only have a few minutes to dedicate to a movement practice. Finally got the kids down for a nap? Hop on YouTube and do a ten-minute yoga or gi gong session. There are also several apps that now offer free classes, so do some research and see which works best for you.**
- **Play! Do something fun that you haven't done since you were a kid. Grab a hula hoop, jump some rope, race your friends up a hill then roll back down. You're never too old to be a kid.**
- **Dance your heart out. Put on your favorite song and just dance. Don't plan it, don't force it, just let your body move how it wants when inspired by the music. Shake out your limbs, kick your feet, flail your arms. Literally, dance like nobody is watching.**

WORRY DUMP

One of the most profound ways you can begin any self-care ritual is relieve your mind of all your swirling, chaotic thoughts. Use the space provided to write down any and all thoughts that have been crowding your mind. Write thoughts that are creating worry and frustration. You don't have to make this pretty; the point is to just write whatever comes to mind and quickly. Something random and unrelated pops into your head? Write it down. Have you been afraid to tell someone off that you're mad at? Write it down. Those deadlines keeping you up at night? Write them down. Nothing is off limits here. Keep your worry stone or a clear quartz crystal nearby to absorb the anxiety and negativity that might arise.

TAKE ACTION

Now that everything is out on the table, read back through your Worry Dump. Many of the things you wrote down are likely out of your control. Alternatively, some of your entries are more than likely something you can act on and resolve.

After your review, list what you can't control. Beside each item, list the crystal that holds properties that you think can help with releasing your need to control the situation.

OUT OF MY CONTROL

1. ______
2. ______
3. ______
4. ______
5. ______
6. ______
7. ______
8. ______
9. ______
10. ______
11. ______
12. ______
13. ______
14. ______
15. ______
16. ______
17. ______
18. ______

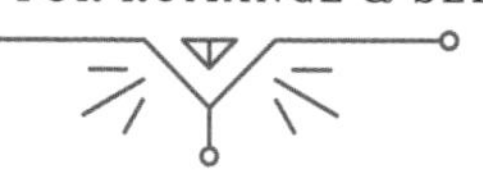

SHIFT YOUR PERSPECTIVE

When things are out of your control, there's very little you can do to change them. What you can do is shift your perspective. For each item on the list of things you can't control, write down one way in which you can make a shift in the way you're seeing the situation. For example, let's say your boss has been significantly more critical of you than usual. You've been working hard and efficiently, but they seem to be inexplicably hard on you. You know you're doing your best so each time they criticize you, you become more and more frustrated and angry. One way you can shift your perspective is to think about what might be going on in their world. It's possible that their boss is being hard on them! Maybe they're facing some deadlines, maybe things are falling apart for them, or maybe they have something happening in their personal life—a sick child, a roof that needs expensive work, a broken-down car. Rather than reacting to their behavior, try to shift your perspective by viewing them through a lens of compassion and curiosity: *I wonder what is making them feel so tightly wound? They shouldn't be treating me like this, but it seems like they are under some kind of pressure, and it must be big because they aren't acting like themselves. What is a small, thoughtful gesture can I do to make their day just a tiny bit brighter?*

In the space below, address each of the items on your list of things you can't control and write about how you can change your perspective. After you do this, you'll likely feel unburdened from stressing about things that you can't change. As you do this, keep crystals near that open your third eye and heart chakras to promote openness and clarity.

TAKE ACTION

Now that you have squared away what you can't control and shifted your perspective, reflect on your Worry Dump and list the things you actually can control. As you do this, keep crystals nearby that hold the properties of motivation, self-confidence, and insight.

WITHIN MY CONTROL

1.
2.
3.
4.
5.
6.
7.
8.
9.
10.
11.
12.
13.
14.
15.
16.
17.
18.
19.
20.

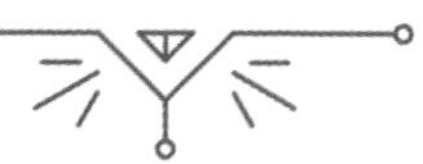

JUST DO IT

Now, looking at the list of things you can control, write about the specific ways that you plan to take action to change them from something worrisome to something that you've actively changed for the better. Then, build a crystal grid that emits positivity, clarity, and compassion to infuse these properties with your own energies as you take positive action.

DEEP RELEASE RITUAL

Even though you've now unburdened yourself, there might be some lingering pain. If you still feel that pang deep inside, perform this ritual to release the pain energy that remains. Imagine sweeping a room of the last bits of dust.

To a warm bath, mindfully add the following ingredients:

* **Epsom salts**
* **Agate for clarity**
* **Rose quartz for an open heart**
* **Amethyst for serenity**
* **A pinch each of the following dried herbs: mint, lemon peel, ground pepper, dried jasmine flowers**
* **10 drops lavender essential oil or to your desired scent strength**

STEP 1

Before climbing into the bath, stir the water with your hands counterclockwise 10 times to raise releasing energy.

STEP 2

Personalize your space. This can mean lighting a candle, putting on meditative music, or placing additional crystals around the tub that you've learned help you clear negativity.

STEP 3

Climb into the bath, take three long, deep, cleansing breaths. Imagine drawing in the power of the crystals and herbs, and breathing out the trapped pain.

STEP 4

As you soak, meditate on the following spell:

I release the pain that crowds my heart.
I release all that is trapped or that I am holding onto.
I release what no longer serves me on my divine path.
I acknowledge my pain.
I allow this water to cleanse and purify my soul.
I forgive myself for reacting to the pain.
I forgive myself for feeling these things.
I am proud myself for taking action.
I'm proud of myself for letting go.
I love myself and I show it.
I love my sensitive heart.
I love my Higher Self.
I am a powerful spirit.
I am free of the hurt and pain.
I am refreshed and energized!
Today starts now.

TAKE ACTION

Working through things that are weighing you down is really the first step to loving and caring for yourself. But it doesn't stop here. Self-care is a daily practice. Taking inspiration from the Deep Release Ritual, list below some of the ways that you perform self-care (or plan to).

1. ....

2. ....

3. ....

4. ....

5. ....

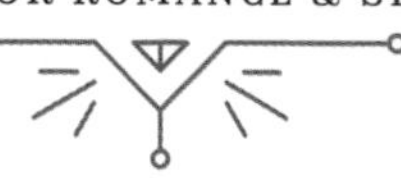

Now, write about how and why you will incorporate crystals into your routines. Be specific about which crystals you will use.

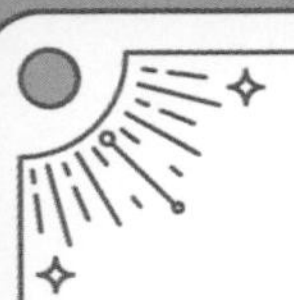

WRITE A LOVE LETTER TO YOURSELF

Although it might feel awkward at first, it's important to give yourself love and encouragement. Push away any self-deprecating thoughts and reflect on all the qualities that make you who you are. Think on your value systems, and praise yourself for your strength of character in upholding these values. Compliment your unique beauty, name and celebrate your attributes (your sense of humor, your compassion, and so on). Write yourself words of encouragement and praise. Give yourself permission to toot your own horn. After you finish, choose a rose quartz to keep with you in a special way. This can be a beautiful necklace or bracelet, maybe it's a heart-shaped rose quartz to remind you to love yourself as you carry it with you, or maybe drop one into a morning cup of tea to sip the energies as you start your day. The options are endless so get creative.

How I will incorporate rose quartz in my daily life as a self-love reminder:

CUTTING TIES

Sometimes, when we're feeling bombarded with negativity, it could be due to the influence of another person's energy. When we enter any type of relationship or engage with a space on a personal level, it is believed that we form an energetic cord that invisibly connects us to an individual or environment. These cords, representing emotional connections, can be a powerful force and become hard to shake when you realize they're not influencing you to be your best self. It may be time to let go and move on, even if you have love for the person or people. It's good to remember that you are never without the option of disengaging from situations and relationships that are no longer positive or loving.

If you've reached a place where it feels like the time has come to release energy and disconnect from some tangled emotions, purifying your space and energy field with the help of incense, sound cleanses, and crystals is a good place to start. Once you have a clear space, you can then begin your work on cutting the energetic cords.

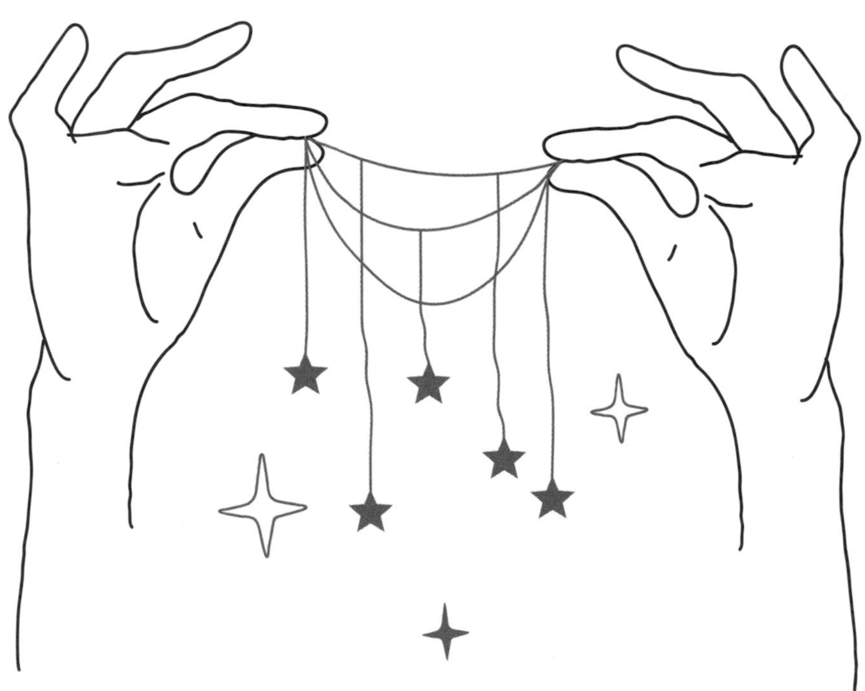

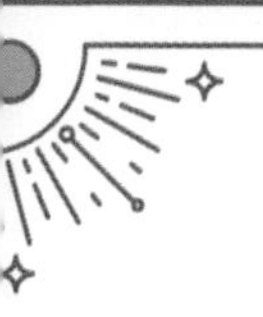

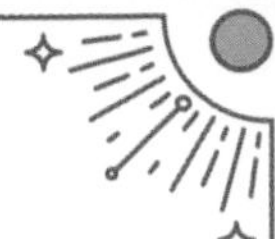

WHO? WHAT? WHERE?

Use the space below to write down who you need to cut ties with, what energy they emit, and where inside you are most affected by them.

Person: ....

Energy: ....

Place inside: ....

Person: ....

Energy: ....

Place inside: ....

Person: ....

Energy: ....

Place inside: ....

Person: ....

Energy: ....

Place inside: ....

Person: ....

Energy: ....

Place inside: ....

CUTTING ENERGY CORDS VISUALIZATION

Most energy cord-cutting techniques utilize black kyanite or obsidian as the cord-cutting element for disengaging negative cords, and amethyst for releasing ties to unhealthy thought patterns. It is also advised that you keep selenite handy for this process to fill energetic gaps with light and positivity, as cord cutting can be energetically jarring.

1. **Cleanse yourself and the space where you will be doing this work using herbs, resins, incense, a salt spray, or a sound cleanse, then do a meditation or breathing exercise.**

2. **Sit in a comfortable position with your eyes closed and think about the person who you need to cut energetic cords with. While holding your chosen crystal in your hand, be mindful of your breathing and where in your physical body the energy feels heavy or blocked.**

3. **Visualize yourself pulling the negative energy out of yourself with a cord.**

4. **In your mind's eye, visualize yourself using your crystal to cut away at these cords, severing their energetic hold on you.**

5. **Watch the loose cords of negativity fall away from you into a positive space; buried in the earth, ascending to the sky, or drifting in a vast ocean.**

6. **In your hand, replace the crystal you used for cutting ties with your selenite. Run the selenite across the areas you visualized removing your cords. Envision those spaces left open after cutting being filled with the light and positivity of the selenite.**

7. **Use this time to express gratitude to the energy that was, the lessons you learned, and the connections you had. This can be done in whatever way feels most genuine to you. *Ho'oponopono*, a Hawaiian prayer that translates to "make things right," can help you release someone while also addressing your own role in the negative-energy exchange. This prayer is a healing mantra to utilize and add strength to any cord-cutting ritual: *I am sorry, please forgive me, thank you, I love you.***

8. **Cleanse the crystals you used, wash the energy from yourself, and hydrate. Take some time to write out your feelings in this moment.**

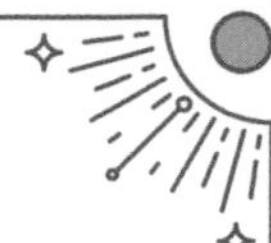

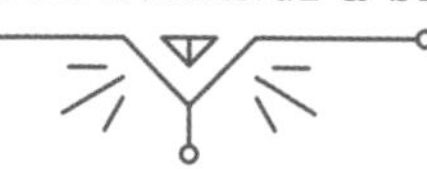

MAKE THINGS RIGHT

In the previous spell, we utilized the Ho'oponopono prayer. As mentioned, this prayer is used to make things right. But this doesn't always resonate with everyone. In order to fully release, forgive, and move forward, we all need a way to look at things from a different angle, and see ourselves through the lens of truth. Sometimes we don't really need to fully cut the cord with people, but we do need to admit where we've been wrong and take action to make things right.

There are always ways we can work to set things right. Begin by referring to your crystal lists and this book, then list the healing crystals that you feel called to use in a healing ritual and how you plan to use them:

1. **Problem area:** ....

   Crystal: ....

   Healing ritual action: ....

2. **Problem area:** ....

   Crystal: ....

   Healing ritual action: ....

3. **Problem area:** ....

   Crystal: ....

   Healing ritual action: ....

4. **Problem area:** ....

   Crystal: ....

   Healing ritual action: ....

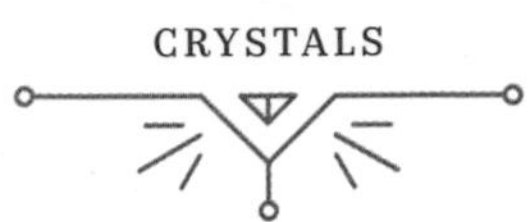

DIG DEEPER

Now, think about your current relationships. Which ones are a little rocky right now? Who have you been disagreeing with that you might need to apologize to? Dig Deep and be honest with yourself.

1. ....

2. ....

3. ....

4. ....

5. ....

6. ....

7. ....

8. ....

9. ....

10. ....

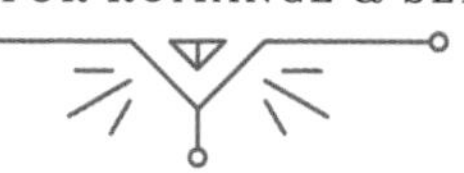

In order to truly live to our potential, it's necessary to forgive. Now that you've identified who you need to forgive, and who might need to forgive you, refer to the following chart to identify forgiveness crystals, their properties, then a suggested use. How you use these crystals is up to you and your intuition, but these should get you started.

CRYSTALS FOR FORGIVENESS

CRYSTAL	PROPERTIES	SUGGESTED USE
Pink Opal	Letting go, calm, hope, healing, emotional balance, love energy	Heart chakra meditation, wear on a pendant near your heart, third eye and heart chakra unblocking ritual, self-care
Rhodonite	Acceptance, balance, compassion, release fear, peace, generosity	Heart and throat chakra meditation, wear on a pendant near your throat, forgiveness grid
Rose Quartz	Unconditional love, nurturing, purifying, acceptance, trust, letting go of pain	Heart chakra meditation, wear on a pendant near your heart, cleansing spray, love ritual, crystal-infused bath, self-care
Unakite Jasper	Emotional balance, release, love, compassion, kindness, uplifting energy, hope	Third-eye chakra meditation, release negativity spells, wear on a bracelet, carry in pocket, forgiveness ritual, place under your pillow
Hiddenite	Healing grief, renewal, love, gratitude, appreciation, joy, spontaneity	Solar plexus meditation, manifesting, any jewelry, carry with you, forgiveness ritual, joy spells, heart chakra cleansing, healing grid

WRITE YOUR OWN FORGIVENESS RITUAL

You have put in the work to emotionally and spiritually identify the issues, the people involved, and which crystals are powerful in assisting forgiveness. Drawing from the rituals and spells you have performed throughout this book, write your own forgiveness ritual. The purpose is to take what you've learned and build a ritual that will help you to let go of pain, resentment, bitterness, and anger and replace these with love, kindness, compassion, and healing. You can create a ritual to forgive yourself or you can focus on forgiving others and releasing what you've been clinging to. This should be whatever speaks to you. Be specific about what crystals you will use in this ritual and what properties they hold that will bolster this process.

conclusion

Thank you for exploring the magic and versatility of crystals with me. After working your way through this book, it is my hope that you've learned something about yourself and how the magic and power of crystals can enhance your life. These ancient formations continue to reveal themselves to scientists, mystics, artists, and enthusiasts, and possess as much value spiritually as they do aesthetically.

Allow the hard work you've done here to be a foundational stepping-stone in your journey of educating yourself about the space that crystals and minerals hold in mystical practice. There is so much more to learn about how they can be incorporated in your daily life and how they provide glimmers of serenity and relief during stressful and draining times. But also, how they can spark joy, romance, self-love, and inner peace. Continue to allow them to illuminate the world around you and nourish your vibrant spirit. We have so much to learn from them, and their bounty is so plentiful that you can spend a whole lifetime digging for deeper understanding and enlightenment.

Use the crystal logs at the end of this book to continue your journey, make notes about new revelations, or to simply record your thoughts and feelings. Revisit this workbook and its exercises periodically, especially when you feel low or in need of some self-love. Continue to make crystal grids, nurture your fairy garden, and press on with your meditations and journaling. Moving your body, eating healthy food, and keeping your spaces clean and organized will all make room for the mystical properties of crystals to refill your energetic coffers. The following pages will help you keep track and set routines to assist you in continuing a successful relationship with your crystals.

May we all continue to dig deeper, to reflect with thoughtful consideration, and retain joyful curiosity, trusting in the dynamic energy of the universe that surrounds us.

CRYSTAL INVENTORY

Crystal:

Properties:

Use:

Water-soluble? ☐ Yes ☐ No

Crystal:

Properties:

Use:

Water-soluble? ☐ Yes ☐ No

Crystal:

Properties:

Use:

Water-soluble? ☐ Yes ☐ No

Crystal:

Properties:

Use:

Water-soluble? ☐ Yes ☐ No

Crystal:

Properties:

Use:

Water-soluble? ☐ Yes ☐ No

Crystal:

Properties:

Use:

Water-soluble? ☐ Yes ☐ No

✦

Crystal:

Properties:

Use:

Water-soluble? ☐ Yes ☐ No

✦

Crystal:

Properties:

Use:

Water-soluble? ☐ Yes ☐ No

✦

Crystal:

Properties:

Use:

Water-soluble? ☐ Yes ☐ No

✦

Crystal:

Properties:

Use:

Water-soluble? ☐ Yes ☐ No

Crystal:

Properties:

Use:

Water-soluble? ☐ Yes ☐ No

Crystal:

Properties:

Use:

Water-soluble? ☐ Yes ☐ No

Crystal:

Properties:

Use:

Water-soluble? ☐ Yes ☐ No

Crystal:

Properties:

Use:

Water-soluble? ☐ Yes ☐ No

Crystal:

Properties:

Use:

Water-soluble? ☐ Yes ☐ No

Crystal:

Properties:

Use:

Water-soluble? ☐ Yes ☐ No

Crystal:

Properties:

Use:

Water-soluble? ☐ Yes ☐ No

Crystal:

Properties:

Use:

Water-soluble? ☐ Yes ☐ No

Crystal:

Properties:

Use:

Water-soluble? ☐ Yes ☐ No

Crystal:

Properties:

Use:

Water-soluble? ☐ Yes ☐ No

CRYSTAL SHAPES LOG

Shape:

Personal associations:

Use:

Shape:

Personal associations:

Use:

Shape:

Personal associations:

Use:

Shape:

Personal associations:

Use:

Shape:

Personal associations:

Use:

Shape:

Personal associations:

Use:

Shape:

Personal associations:

Use:

Shape:

Personal associations:

Use:

Shape:

Personal associations:

Use:

Shape:

Personal associations:

Use:

Shape:

Personal associations:

Use:

Shape:

Personal associations:

Use:

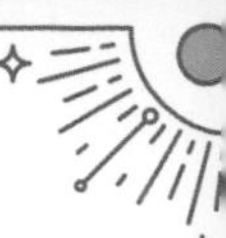

CLEANSING TOOLKIT INVENTORY

Cleansing tool:

Energy it clears:

Source:

Frequency of use:

Description of scent:

Cleansing tool:

Energy it clears:

Source:

Frequency of use:

Description of scent:

Cleansing tool:

Energy it clears:

Source:

Frequency of use:

Description of scent:

Cleansing tool:

Energy it clears:

Source:

Frequency of use:

Description of scent:

Cleansing tool: ____________________

Energy it clears: ____________________

Source: ____________________

Frequency of use: ____________________

Description of scent: ____________________

Cleansing tool: ____________________

Energy it clears: ____________________

Source: ____________________

Frequency of use: ____________________

Description of scent: ____________________

Cleansing tool: ____________________

Energy it clears: ____________________

Source: ____________________

Frequency of use: ____________________

Description of scent: ____________________

Cleansing tool: ____________________

Energy it clears: ____________________

Source: ____________________

Frequency of use: ____________________

Description of scent: ____________________

CLEANSING LOG

Crystal: ....

Date: ....

Moon phase/event: ....

Method of cleanse: ....

Crystal: ....

Date: ....

Moon phase/event: ....

Method of cleanse: ....

Crystal: ....

Date: ....

Moon phase/event: ....

Method of cleanse: ....

Crystal: ....

Date: ....

Moon phase/event: ....

Method of cleanse: ....

Crystal: ....

Date: ....

Moon phase/event: ....

Method of cleanse: ....

Crystal:

Date:

Moon phase/event:

Method of cleanse:

Crystal:

Date:

Moon phase/event:

Method of cleanse:

Crystal:

Date:

Moon phase/event:

Method of cleanse:

Crystal:

Date:

Moon phase/event:

Method of cleanse:

Crystal:

Date:

Moon phase/event:

Method of cleanse:

PROGRAMMING LOG

Date:

Crystal:

Intention:

Date:

Crystal:

Intention:

Date:

Crystal:

Intention:

Date:

Crystal:

Intention:

Date:

Crystal:

Intention:

Date:

Crystal:

Intention:

Date:

Crystal:

Intention:

Date:

Crystal:

Intention:

Date:

Crystal:

Intention:

Date:

Crystal:

Intention:

Date:

Crystal:

Intention:

Date:

Crystal:

Intention:

UNBLOCKING LOG

Chakra:

Unblocking crystals:

Chakra:

Unblocking crystals:

Chakra:

Unblocking crystals:

Chakra:

Unblocking crystals:

Chakra:

Unblocking crystals:

Chakra:

Unblocking crystals:

Chakra:

Unblocking crystals:

Chakra:

Unblocking crystals:

Chakra:

Unblocking crystals:

Chakra:

Unblocking crystals:

Chakra:

Unblocking crystals:

Chakra:

Unblocking crystals:

Chakra:

Unblocking crystals:

Chakra:

Unblocking crystals:

Chakra:

Unblocking crystals:

Chakra:

Unblocking crystals:

DREAM JOURNAL

Date:

Crystal used:

Dream and emotion experienced:

Date:

Crystal used:

Dream and emotion experienced:

Date:

Crystal used:

Dream and emotion experienced:

Date:

Crystal used:

Dream and emotion experienced:

Date:

Crystal used:

Dream and emotion experienced:

Date:

Crystal used:

Dream and emotion experienced:

Date:

Crystal used:

Dream and emotion experienced:

Date:

Crystal used:

Dream and emotion experienced:

First published in 2023 by Wellfleet, an imprint of The Quarto Group,
142 West 36th Street, 4th Floor, New York, NY 10018, USA
T (212) 779-4972 F (212) 779-6058
www.Quarto.com

10 9 8 7 6 5 4 3 2 1

ISBN: 978-1-57715-352-8

Publisher: Rage Kindelsperger
Creative Director: Laura Drew
Managing Editor: Cara Donaldson
Editor: Sara Bonacum
Cover and Interior Design: Verso Design

Printed in China

This book provides general information on crystals and positive spiritual habits. However, it should not be relied upon as recommending or promoting any specific diagnosis or method of treatment for a particular condition, and it is not intended as a substitute for medical advice or for direct diagnosis and treatment of a medical condition by a qualified physician. Readers who have questions about a particular condition, possible treatments for that condition, or possible reactions from the condition or its treatment should consult a physician or other qualified healthcare professional.